Atheists in the Afterlife

Eight Paths to Life After Death Without God

D1516210

Sea Kimbrell

DEDICATION

For my children.

CONTENTS

CHAPTER 1

INTRODUCTION

At first it seems completely obvious—of course there can be no afterlife without a deity to create it. If God does not exist, then it would be ludicrous to expect life after death. The entire reason for this book is to suggest that what seems obvious may be utterly wrong. Each chapter presents a different way in which the afterlife may exist, even if God does not. Moreover, every possible route to the afterlife discussed in this book has been proposed or refined by well-respected scientists and philosophers.

You may immediately suspect that I will be describing an afterlife only for those humans who live far in the future, when technology such as the ability to upload a brain into a computer becomes possible. While I will briefly discuss brain uploading in a later chapter, the thesis of this book is that the afterlife may exist for every human who has ever lived, in the past and the future, and very much including every person alive right now.

Before worrying about the afterlife, though, we might ask why we should even bother caring about life after death in the first place—after all, shouldn't this life be enough? The idea that our time on Earth is plenty certainly seems to be an oft-repeated sentiment. I will embarrassedly admit that whenever I'm feeling bored or listless, I like to read quotes by people more brilliant and insightful than me. I always hope that the right combination of words and sentiments will fill me with renewed inspiration. Not surprisingly, given its importance to all of us, many of the quotes I find are about death or dying. A large percentage of those quotes confidently assert that you won't fear death, or even be saddened by it, if you live a full life. For instance, Leonardo da Vinci is credited as saying, "As a well-spent day brings happy sleep, so a life well spent brings happy death;" while Anaïs Nin wrote, "People living deeply have no fear of death." As inspiring as those quotes are, I think they're complete rubbish.

Consider the example of Doris Lamar-McLemore. A teacher and housemother at an American Indian boarding school, she died on August 30, 2016, at the age of eighty-nine. She certainly lived fully and deeply, and was remembered fondly by her family and her community. It was not who remembered her, though, but what she remembered that makes her so important. Ms. Lamar-McLemore was the last fluent speaker of the Wichita language—a language that had been spoken by tribal groups across the Great Plains of the United States for thousands of years. While recordings exist of Ms. Lamar-McLemore speaking Wichita, her death brought the extinction of the Wichita language. We should allow ourselves to feel sad at realizing that after being a living language for thousands of years, no song, story, or poem will ever again be composed in the Wichita tongue.

As the example of Ms. Lamar-McLemore suggests, we each write the story of our life in our own language. You are the only person fluent in the intricacies and unexpected grammar of your existence. While you are alive, your life writes thousands of stories, songs, and poems. Do those stories end when you die? Does the language of your life become extinct? No matter how many wonderful stories you wrote while alive, the possibility that no more will ever be written absolutely demands fear and sadness. No one should consider it unseemly or pathetic to be saddened by the thought of his or her own death, of the possible end of the language of one's life.

Sadness at the thought of death, though, naturally leads to a hope that perhaps our language does not end when we take our last breath. Many of us want to believe that somehow, someway, our minds will find their way to composing new stories and poems and songs. We want to believe in the afterlife.

Most major religions are quite happy to promise just such an afterlife. In the religious version of life after death, a god or gods gives every living person a soul (or some other supernatural element) that animates the lump of molecules we call bodies. After death the soul leaves the body, often transported away from Earth on

Figure 1. Some of us might choose to skip heaven if it means being ordered around by horrifying angel-babies for eternity. *Three Angels on Clouds*, by Bernardino Luini, c. 1515-18. Public domain.

some celestial highway. The soul retains all the thoughts and memories of the person from before death and continues to think and feel after leaving the body. The soul then enters some special place set aside by God, where all the other departed souls reside, and exists in this special realm for eternity. In the religious afterlife, you get to spend eternity sitting on a white cloud while strumming a harp and listening to angels sing the hymnal version of *Stairway to Heaven* (see Figure 1).

Many of us, though, don't believe in the existence of God, and certainly don't believe in any organized religion. We have given ourselves over to a seemingly harsh reality—that no God exists to grant us life after death. While we may not believe in a god, that doesn't mean we particularly like the idea of our consciousness disappearing forever as we take our last breath. Even most of us who are atheists would like to believe that our minds will somehow survive the deaths of our bodies. As I've already suggested, though, most everyone assumes that the existence of the afterlife depends on the existence of a God willing to create such an afterlife. If you don't believe in God, it would seem you are out of luck.

This obviously presents a pretty big problem for anyone who doesn't believe in God—constant existential dread at one's own coming oblivion is not a fun way to live (and makes one pretty tiresome during family vacations). The good news is that we need not despair! As the following chapters will explain, there are several scientific and philosophical reasons to believe that consciousness does not end with death.

Regrettably, many of these ideas are not known to the general public. As the major religions have already staked their claim to the afterlife, scientists and most philosophers view any serious consideration of the subject off-limits. Consequently, the scientific and philosophical evidence pointing to some form of the afterlife aren't discussed much within the academic community. As this book will show, however, even though there may not be a god, there is considerable scientific and philosophical evidence pointing to the existence of an afterlife. Indeed, the language of your life may very well continue after you die — allowing stories, songs, and poetry to be written for eternity.

What This Book Is About

This book presents eight arguments that scientists and philosophers have put forth to suggest the possibility of life after death. These arguments for the afterlife do not rely on the current existence of a god. I do my best to present the arguments in as simple and straightforward a manner as possible while still doing justice to the underlying scientific and philosophical ideas. I also attempt to present the arguments as objectively as possible, pointing out any weaknesses in the reasoning.

Given the speculative nature of any book about the afterlife, you may find some of the arguments in these chapters more persuasive than others. I personally find a few of the ideas very convincing, while others seem extremely unlikely. You may very well sigh with exasperation at a handful of the ideas presented in this book.

My intention, though, remains to present all the scientific and philosophical arguments for the afterlife in the absence of a God, no matter how seemingly unlikely. I describe the persuasive and not-so-persuasive ideas with equal attention, confident that what one person finds compelling another will find laughable, and vice versa. I have no desire, however, to place probabilities on which arguments in the book are most likely to be true. That task must be done by each reader alone. Hopefully, after reading this book, you will find that at least a few of the arguments for the afterlife are downright convincing, and will set the book down with a newfound belief in the possibility of life after death.

What This Book Is Not About

This book is not about trying to prove that God does not exist. Most people reading this book have likely already made up their minds in one direction or the other. If not, there are plenty of nonfiction works by philosophers and scientists that do a good job of illustrating the lack of proof for the existence of God. A good treatment of such arguments, with a fairly heavy emphasis on scientific theory, may be found in *The God Delusion* by Richard Dawkins. A more philosophical take resides in *The Non-Existence of God* by Nicholas Everitt.

If, on the other hand, you are interested in the arguments meant to prove the existence of God, there are a multitude of options. I recommend starting with, *Is There a God?* by Richard Swinburne. I'm afraid I don't find any of Swinburne's arguments persuasive. I do think, however, that there is value in reading and understanding the reasoning of those you disagree with (even if you do start to notice all the cracks in your ceiling because you are spending so much time rolling your eyes).

Who This Book Is For

I certainly hope a wide range of people with a broad scope of beliefs read this book. I am confident that the book demonstrates that our intuitive understanding of the universe is frequently contradicted by scientific experiments and simple logic. If we don't understand the true nature of reality, then perhaps we don't understand the true nature of death.

As described in more detail in the next section, I broke this book into two parts. The first half of the book examines the scientific evidence for the afterlife, while the second half provides the philosophical arguments for life after death. I will admit that in my training as a scientist, I found little use for philosophical reasoning. However, in researching and writing this book, I found the arguments of the philosophers to lead to fascinating insights that scientists tend to ignore because of the difficulty in testing them experimentally. While philosophers tend not to perform as many scientific experiments as physicists, the disciplined reasoning of philosophers provides important insights into our understanding of the cosmos. I hope that those readers who are more scientifically inclined will take the time to seriously engage with the philosophical ideas in the second half of the book. At the same time, I hope the more philosophically disposed will find the scientific ideas in the first half of the book to provide experimental grounding for our understanding of reality.

As the title suggests, this book was written primarily with atheists and agnostics in mind. The people who have come to the conclusion that God likely does not exist tend to fall into two categories: 1) those who believe that modern science shows no evidence for the existence of God, and therefore no need for Him; and 2) those who take a more philosophical view of the universe, and find that reason and logic provide no refuge for God to hide in. Obviously, those same conclusions can be hurled at the existence of the afterlife. Hopefully, by the end of the book, readers will find that scientific evidence does exist for the afterlife, and life after death does indeed find support in logic and reason.

There may be some people reading this book, however, who do believe in God. I sincerely hope that such readers will find value in these pages. The sacred texts of most major religions state that God will provide believers with an afterlife. Those texts, however, tend to be extremely vague on exactly what form that afterlife will take. Anyone reading this book who believes in God should consider that maybe the afterlife discussed in the sacred texts was meant to take one of the forms discussed in this book. If God does exist, perhaps a version of life after death outlined in one of the following chapters is exactly what He meant by the afterlife.

Finally, this book is aimed squarely at anyone who doubts that the reality we see before our eyes, or learn about in the structured environment of the classroom, contains all that exists. Many of the potential versions of the afterlife presented in the following chapters are not mutually exclusive. In other words, it may be possible that your consciousness will continue to exist after death in several different ways. How fascinating, and potentially scary, that while you are alive there is only one version of your consciousness, but after death there may exist two, three, or more versions of your conscious mind—each version existing independently and completely unaware of the others. Death may not be the end of your conscious mind, but the point at which it expands to reside simultaneously in several new realities. There may be not one afterlife, but many!

Roadmap

Despite what religious leaders may say, arriving at the afterlife doesn't require a roadmap. A map, however, can be pretty useful for navigating the ideas in a book. Following this brief introduction, the book moves on to eight substantive chapters, each one describing a different path to the afterlife, as well as a concluding chapter that tries to tie everything together. A few of the substantive chapters actually contain several separate arguments for the afterlife, but the different ideas are each related to the main theme of the chapter, and I thought it best to lump them together in the same chapter.

Chapters two through five take a scientific approach to the question of life after death. These first four substantive chapters focus on scientific theories, arising mostly from the field of physics, that suggest ways in which an afterlife may occur. The chapters explore how experiments at the edge of our understanding of the universe point to the possibility of life after death. The versions of the afterlife discussed in these chapters have been endorsed by some of the greatest physicists of the last century.

Chapters six through nine take a more philosophical view of the afterlife. These four chapters examine the arguments proposed by philosophers as providing proof for the existence of life after death. The emphasis on philosophy in these four chapters means that the book is almost evenly split between scientific and philosophical arguments for the afterlife. Hopefully, the insights of both science and philosophy will lead to a clearer understanding of whether or not the afterlife truly exists.

Listed below are brief descriptions of the eight paths to life after death, along with a description of the concluding chapter. Feel free to skip directly to any chapter that catches your fancy or seems the most intriguing. Some of the later chapters refer to ideas discussed in earlier chapters, but I'll wager you'll be able to figure out what's going on. The next nine chapters in the book are:

Chapter 2: Simulating the Afterlife

Basic probability suggests that we are more likely to be simulated creations than flesh and blood. If we truly are the products of a computer program, will those responsible for creating our digital minds feel a duty to give us eternal life?

Chapter 3:   Block Universe

We have no trouble believing that space far away from us still exists, even if we can't see or touch it. Why do we assume that time is any different? A century of physics experiments suggests that each second in time exists simultaneously. Every moment in the universe—both in the past and in the future—is just as real as the present moment. This means that every moment of your life exists simultaneously for eternity.

Chapter 4:   The Entangled Life

So far, there are no scientific theories that convincingly explain human consciousness. One hypothesis that appears promising, though, argues that entangled quantum particles within the brain give rise to consciousness. Some proponents of this hypothesis then take the next step and suggest that the entangled states of the brain continue to exist after death. Remaining in the quantum realm, the chapter also explores how quantum phenomena may predict an afterlife within a multiverse of constantly branching universes.

Chapter 5:   Uploading the Dead

If it ever becomes possible for a future human civilization to peer into the past, what will they do first? Reincarnating every human who has ever lived, through digital or other means, seems a very real possibility.

Chapter 6:   Open Individualism

Ever since philosophers started calling themselves philosophers, they have struggled to come to terms with the most difficult problems of reality, such as how does an individual retain her identity even as she constantly changes through time? The concept of open individualism tackles the vexing problem of the continuity of the self by suggesting that while we each have different bodies, only a single animating force gives rise to each of our conscious minds. While our bodies may die, this universal consciousness never dies.

Chapter 7:   A Soul without a God

Based solely on logic, no contradiction arises from the idea that the soul exists, but that God does not exist. In fact, the philosophical evidence for the existence of the soul is much more persuasive than the philosophical evidence for the existence of God.

Chapter 8:   Reincarnation and the Deterministic Universe

Much of the desire for an afterlife resides in the fear that this life does not have any lasting meaning. If the universe is deterministic, though, then your existence became inevitable at the moment of the big bang, and each thought you have, and every action you undertake, will continue to directly influence the evolution of the universe for the rest of time.

Chapter 9:   God Does Not Exist . . . Yet

Most major religions hold as a basic tenet that God created the universe. But what if they have it backward—what if the universe will eventually create God? No proof exists that God inhabits the universe now, but perhaps God will pop into existence in the future. We should not be at all surprised if such a newly created deity decided to resurrect the minds of all the creatures who had ever lived.

Chapter 10:   Conclusions

In this chapter I attempt to tie all the previous chapters up in a nice bow, while simultaneously dispensing profound wisdom and sketching out a grand unified theory of the meaning of life. I, of course, fail spectacularly. Not surprisingly, life and death are extremely messy, and will continue to be so until no conscious mind in the universe remains to ponder their tricky relationship. All I can hope to achieve in the final chapter of this book is to convince you that the preceding chapters present reasonable paths to the afterlife, and that maybe, just maybe, we will all meet again in a life after this one.

CHAPTER 2

SIMULATING THE AFTERLIFE

The Japanese toymaker Bandai released the Tamagotchi on November 23, 1996. An inauspicious lump of plastic, the Tamagotchi was a palm-sized oval with a small pixelated screen. As Figure 2 shows, the Tamagotchi looks like the type of cheap prize you would get from your dentist when you were a kid and didn't scream when she brought out the drill.

Upon activating the Tamagotchi, an egg would appear on the digital screen, and from this egg would hatch an alien-like creature. This alien baby would be hungry and need to be digitally fed. If fed enough to keep its hunger bar full, the alien would grow into a child, then a teen, and finally an adult. To keep the adult alien happy, the Tamagotchi owner would have to play games with it, give it medicine when it was sick, and clean up its digital droppings. All this was done by pressing three little buttons on the front of the toy. The

Figure 2. A Tamagotchi toy, illustrating the luck of kids who grew up with smart phones. Tomasz Sienicki, CC BY-SA.

entire point of the Tamagotchi was to keep the digital creature on the screen alive—if the person playing with the Tamagotchi didn't perform the required tasks, the little alien would die.

Amazingly, the Tamagotchi became one of the biggest toy fads of the late 1990s and early 2000s. Between 1996 and 2017, Bandai sold more than eighty-two million Tamagotchis. Chances are, if you were a child around the turn of the millennium (or were the parent of such a child), you had a Tamagotchi.

During the height of the fad, droves of children brought their Tamagotchis to school. A newspaper article from 1997 described how the Tamagotchis caused classroom disruption as students checked on their digital aliens every few minutes.[1] A teacher quoted in the article voiced astonishment that third-grade students were more interested in their digital aliens than in taking a standardized exam, saying, "[t]he children were more concerned with the toy than with succeeding in the test." I will refrain from making any comments about a teacher being surprised by third graders showing more interest in toys than standardized tests.

As a result of the mayhem caused by students checking on their Tamagotchis during school hours, many schools across the United States banned the toy. Some students continued to sneak their Tamagotchis into school, though, willing to risk the wrath of their teachers. The students took such huge risks because they were rightfully afraid that if they left their digital aliens alone for an entire school day the pets would die.

The (perhaps irrational) desire to care for something we helped create shouldn't come as a shock. To many of those who owned a Tamagotchi, the digital creatures they were keeping alive on the pixelated screen were nearly as real as any flesh-and-blood pet. Not surprisingly, the kids playing with their Tamagotchis would do anything to avoid the deaths of their beloved digital creations. Although they were only children, the owners of the Tamagotchis almost certainly understood that their little aliens were merely pixels on a screen and not real creatures. Consider, though, how the Tamagotchis' owners would have felt if they had known with certainty that their digital pets were conscious. How would they have reacted if they had known that the little aliens could feel real hunger and pain? To what lengths would they have gone to prevent the deaths of their digital pets?

I raise these questions because they bear directly on the likelihood that humans will receive an afterlife. I realize that the Tamagotchi toy and the afterlife seem to have absolutely no connection whatsoever, but they are in fact intimately related. As this chapter will argue, there is a high probability that this world and every single human in it exist as a simulation in a computer model. If this is true, then how we think about and treat our digital creations may determine whether we experience life after death. If it turns out we are simulated beings—little more than slightly advanced descendants of a Tamagotchi alien—a great deal depends on whether third graders find us more interesting than standardized tests.

Simulated Humans

At first the whole idea seems laughable—of course we're real beings and not simulated creations! Amazingly, the argument that we are not flesh-and-blood humans, but instead digital creations, has probability on its side.

Scientists currently use computer models to simulate all kinds of different phenomena in the hopes of understanding them better. For instance, there are simulations of the animals in ecosystems, the movement of financial markets, and the electricity coursing through power grids. There are also hundreds upon hundreds of simulations of digital humans. The digital humans in these simulations are extremely simple — usually just a few programmed characteristics a researcher hopes will interact in interesting ways. Despite their simplicity, though, the digital humans frequently produce interesting patterns in the models, often replicating real-world phenomena such as voting decisions or immigration patterns.

The humans in these simulations are nowhere close to being conscious — they consist of nothing more than a few lines of computer code. But we shouldn't expect matters to remain this way forever. In the future, scientists will almost certainly be able to create simulated humans that are so realistic that they replicate every thought, behavior, and action of a living human. If a simulated human can replicate us in every way, then surely it can replicate our consciousness as well.

I pause here to briefly consider the nature of consciousness. As subsequent chapters will discuss in greater detail, some scientists and philosophers believe that human consciousness cannot be explained by our present understanding of physics and biology. They argue that consciousness requires either a physical theory that has yet to be discovered, or a metaphysical explanation that suggests the existence of a soul. These are by far the minority views. The vast majority of scientists and philosophers believe that human consciousness, while not yet fully understood, will eventually be explained through our current understanding of the physical laws of nature. This shouldn't be particularly controversial — if human consciousness is the result of roughly eighty-six billion neurons interacting, at some point a computer program should be complex enough to simulate each one of those eighty-six billion cells. When that occurs, a truly conscious mind should exist within the computer. For the purposes of this chapter, then, I will assume that eventually scientists will be able to digitally simulate human consciousness.

Why go to the trouble of creating conscious humans in a computer simulation? The answer is simple: The better the simulation, the better the predictions. If a scientist wants to understand a phenomenon that depends on complex human decision-making, such as who to vote for in an election or whether to eat the last slice of pie now or tomorrow for breakfast, he will want to simulate that decision-making as perfectly as possible. Humans are conscious beings, so perfectly simulated humans would also need to be conscious. In other words, the desire to understand our universe will almost inevitably lead to the desire to perfectly emulate the universe inside a computer. The best way to understand human behavior will be to create conscious humans in a computer and watch how they interact.

When scientists working today create their simplified simulations of human behavior, they usually run each simulation hundreds or thousands of times. They do this because they are interested in varying parts of the simulation and then seeing how changing one part of the model changes the outcome of the simulation. These parts of the simulation that are varied between runs of the model are called parameters. For example, a scientist might decide to vary the parameter determining the probability that voters will be influenced by a political candidate's position on eating pie for breakfast. The scientist would run the model many times, with different values for the parameter, from no voters caring about pie to every single voter caring deeply. The scientist would then watch how changes in the value of the parameter alter the outcomes of the simulation.

Most simulations have dozens, and often hundreds, of parameters. The scientist who created the model would likely want to vary each one of those parameters to determine how they change the outcomes of the simulation. This means varying one parameter while all the others are held constant, then moving on to the next parameter, varying it while holding the others constant. The scientist would need to do that for every possible combination of parameters. As a result, if a scientist has created a complex simulation, she will need to run the model hundreds of times to account for all the possible parameter combinations.

Amazingly, this accounts for only some of the necessary simulation runs. For each parameter, a scientist running the model will need to use a random number generator to determine how the parameter applies to the simulated people in the model. For instance, a parameter in the model might state that 20 percent of simulated people are influenced by a political candidate's position on pie for breakfast. A random number generator would then determine whether a person in the simulation falls within that 20 percent or not. For each combination of parameters, the simulation must be run hundreds of times to allow the scientist to average over the random numbers. Only then can the people who created the simulation figure out the most likely outcomes. As should be evident, scientists must run complex computer simulations thousands of times to understand the patterns produced by those simulations. This need to run computer models so many times is important because it determines the probability of our being flesh-and-blood humans.

In 2003, the Oxford University philosopher Nick Bostrom had an ingenious insight. He began as above by assuming that in the future, scientists will almost certainly be able to simulate human consciousness. Given this ability, researchers will begin to simulate human consciousness to help model complex systems, such as societies and political movements and the lines to buy beer at sporting events. The simulations that the scientists create will need to resemble the physical world as closely as possible to be of any value. Consequently, the conscious minds created in the simulations would need to be kept in the dark that they are part of a computer simulation. In other words, the simulated humans would need to believe that they exist in the physical universe, not merely a simulated one.

Like the scientists working on simulation models today, scientists in the future will need to run their models thousands upon thousands of times to provide any useful understanding of their simulated worlds. Each one of those simulations might include millions of conscious digital humans. This means that in the future we should expect hundreds or thousands of scientists, running thousands or hundreds of thousands of simulations, containing millions or billions of conscious humans. The end result of all this will be the creation of trillions of digital conscious minds, with each one believing it exists in the real world.

We now have a comparison to make: As far as we know, there is only one real physical universe; on the other hand, in the future, scientists will almost certainly create millions of simulated worlds. We can expect the researchers will do their best to make sure the humans in the simulations don't realize they are in a simulation, believing instead they are in the physical universe. As Nick Bostrom grasped, the comparison is clear—if there are millions of simulated worlds with conscious beings, but only one physical universe with conscious beings, then we are much more likely to be simulated humans in a computer model than real humans in the physical world. To put this another way, the future may have already arrived in the physical universe, and the universe you and I are in right now is one of the millions of simulated universes the physical scientists of the future have created.

But It Feels Real

The most obvious objection to the idea that we are simulated beings is that the world seems so real. No scientist, philosopher, or random beachcomber with a metal detector has ever found any evidence that we inhabit a simulated world. Intuitively, it seems unlikely that a computer would be capable of simulating an entire world so flawlessly.

There are two reasons why a computer simulation of the world may seem flawless. First, any human that has been created by a scientist to exist in a simulation may have been programmed to believe that the world seems perfectly real and perfectly flawless. Perhaps we have been specifically designed not to notice the seams in the universe. Second, the world may seem perfectly real because it has been designed solely for you.

So far, this chapter has assumed that any computer model of the world would contain millions of simulated human minds. Maybe some scientists in the future, though, will have different interests. Perhaps they will want to simulate how one human reacts to a range of different scenarios. We must consider the possibility that you are the only truly conscious individual in the entire simulated universe. Scientists may have created the entire world to observe how your mind reacts to each new and increasingly outlandish event. The scientists programming such a simulation would make sure that wherever you go, wherever you look, whatever action you take, the model world would replicate the real world down to the smallest detail. The end result would be that only you are truly conscious, while everyone else is a zombie designed to imitate the existence of conscious thought behind dead eyes.

Of course, the opposite may also be true. The possibility exists that some other simulated individual is the true interest of the scientists who have created this universe, and you have been made just convincing enough to fool yourself into believing that you are a real person. Perhaps everyone reading this book are zombies, meant to fool someone else into thinking this simulated world is the physical universe.

If the thought of being nothing more than a barely thinking background character in someone else's simulation seems existentially depressing, hope remains. As Descartes famously wrote, "I think therefore I am." If you are able to experience your own consciousness—if you are aware of your own mind—then you are truly conscious. Your consciousness may not be as impressive or fully developed as the person who happens to be the focus of the simulation, but as long as you can think and feel then you are more than a meaningless background character. If you can hear your own mind, then you truly are more than just a few lines of computer code.

Regardless of whether you are the star of the show, a supporting player, or one of a billion equally conscious minds, the above arguments still apply. Based on simply probability, your conscious mind is more likely to have been born in a computer simulation than in the physical universe.

What Does This Mean For The Afterlife?

To decide what this means for the possibility of life after death, we must accept that we may be digital guinea pigs, created to help answer a scientific question.

We can then look at how we currently treat conscious beings that do not know they are experimental subjects—specifically, we can look at chimpanzees used in biomedical experiments.

In 1960, the United States government created a series of primate centers to conduct biomedical research on chimpanzees. Some of the chimpanzees were bred in captivity, but most were taken from Africa. By 1973, the US had stopped importing chimpanzees from Africa, but continued to breed them in captivity. Approximately twenty years later, there were more than 1,500 chimpanzees in US research labs.

Beginning in the 1990s, though, popular opinion on using chimpanzees in biomedical experiments began to change. Many scientists and philosophers had begun to argue that chimpanzees have a level of consciousness similar to our own; consequently, they reasoned, invasive biomedical experiments on chimpanzees are just as unethical as the same biomedical experiments on humans. Many people came to the conclusion that experiments on the great apes should be banned.

In response, the National Institutes of Health began to phase out support for chimpanzee biomedical research in 2013. Biomedical research continued, though, until 2015. In that year, the US Fish and Wildlife Service finally declared chimpanzees an endangered species, thereby officially ending biomedical research on the apes.

Once the biomedical experiments on chimpanzees had ended, there remained the question of what to do with all the apes still in labs. Captive chimpanzees usually live to more than thirty years of age, with some living past the age of sixty. The research labs were no longer able to use the chimpanzees in experiments, so they saw no reason to keep the chimpanzees around — they took up valuable space and cost money to feed. The chimpanzees could not be released into the wild, as they had lived in captivity their entire lives and would have no chance of surviving in their natural habitats.

By far, the easiest and least expensive option would have been to humanely put each of the chimpanzees to sleep. After all, the chimpanzees had served their purpose as experimental animals, and now that those experiments were no longer allowed it made no logical sense to keep the chimpanzees alive.

Fortunately, that notion was completely rejected. Instead, the US government created a sanctuary for chimpanzees called Chimp Haven. Existing as a nonprofit preserve, the designers hoped to reproduce an idyllic version of the apes' natural habitat. Other groups created additional nonprofit chimpanzee sanctuaries, also attempting to replicate an idyllic version of nature. At each of the sanctuaries, the chimpanzees have space to explore, are given food and medical attention, and get to live out the rest of their lives in relative peace. To compensate the chimpanzees who had been used in biomedical experiments against their will, they were rewarded with an ape version of paradise.

No matter your personal belief about scientific testing on animals, I think it safe to write that in general, humans value the consciousness of other beings. Out of this springs distaste at the thought of allowing a conscious being such as a chimpanzee to be used for scientific experimentation and then thrown away. We could have simply put the chimpanzees to sleep when they were no longer scientifically useful, but instead we provided them with an approximation of chimpanzee heaven.

Of course, the chimpanzees in the sanctuaries are as real (or perhaps unreal) as we are. Would we care about digital chimpanzees? The story of the Tamagotchi in the introduction suggests we would. Humans seem inclined to think of digital creatures as being almost as real as living creatures. If we created digital chimpanzees that were truly conscious, I imagine most people would want them to be moved to a digital sanctuary when they were no longer part of an experiment.

Certainly, the same would hold true for any human minds created in a simulation. If scientists in the future simulate conscious minds that exactly replicate physical human minds, it seems very unlikely that they will simply use those simulated minds in scientific experiments and then discard them. To do so would be like putting real humans to sleep after they finished their part in a biomedical experiment.

The revulsion at throwing away conscious minds may lead future civilizations to outlaw the simulation of human minds all together, much as we have outlawed biomedical research on chimpanzees. This also seems unlikely, though. The understanding of the world that would come about from simulating conscious human minds would be enormous. The National Institutes of

Health decided to phase out funding for research on chimpanzees because their scientists determined that experiments on mice would provide just as much scientific information as experiments on chimpanzees. The same would not be true for simulations of human consciousness. Only by simulating human minds could scientists hope to understand complex human behavior. Experiments on mice yield important information about human physiology; experiments on mice yield very little information about human art, culture, or politics. Much more likely, the civilizations of the future will allow scientists to simulate conscious human minds. However, in return, they will likely pass laws requiring that any scientist who simulates human consciousness for use in an experiment must compensate that consciousness in some way.

The most obvious way to compensate a conscious mind forced to exist as an experiment in a computer simulation is to reward that mind with an idyllic life after it dies in the experiment. Put another way, we should expect that any human mind created in a computer will be rewarded with a simulated heaven.

In practice, this means that after a simulated mind has completed his or her role in the model and died in the simulation, his or her consciousness will be automatically moved over to a simulated afterlife. If the arguments above are true—if simulated humans vastly outnumber physical humans and we are more likely simulated humans than physical humans—then the afterlife will be all of ours. Given what we know about human behavior and morality, perhaps we can even make an educated guess about what the simulated afterlife will look like.

Simulating Heaven

Most likely, we'll be treated about the same as the chimpanzees used in scientific experiments. After we die in the simulation, our consciousness will probably be transferred to a new computer—call it *Chip Haven*. We should expect to be treated to an idyllic existence, with no pain, no hunger, and no need to work or pay bills. Every imaginable type of food and entertainment should be plentiful and free. We will die in the simulation and wake up in what can only be described as heaven. Just like the chimpanzees in Chimp Haven, Chip Haven will be our compensation for being brought into existence as unwilling test subjects.

As mentioned above, many of the existing chimpanzee sanctuaries are run as independent nonprofit organizations. Similarly, we might expect Chip Haven to be run as an independent organization. Such an organization would likely offer its services as a provider of the afterlife for many different universities and research institutions. Each university or lab would pay Chip Haven a monthly fee to provide afterlife services for the human minds it had created.

Unfortunately, Chip Haven may share some other, less desirable, similarities with the chimpanzee sanctuaries. The chimpanzees used in biomedical experiments were placed in seemingly idyllic sanctuaries, but those sanctuaries did have fences. The apes in their Gardens of Eden were not completely free—they were forced to remain within the confines of their reward. More troublingly, since being transferred to the sanctuaries, there have been several investigative reports on the conditions of those sanctuaries.[2] The reporting shows that many of the sanctuaries are not well funded, and the chimpanzees do not have the serene life hyped in the early press releases. The primary reason stems from the universities and labs wanting to pay the sanctuaries as little as possible to care for the chimpanzees. Of course, this shouldn't be surprising—research institutions want to spend as much money as possible on new research experiments (or pay raises for university administrators), and as little as possible on the upkeep of their former research subjects.

If we are indeed research subjects likely to be rewarded with life after death, the afterlife we find ourselves in may be free of pain and disease, but not very imaginatively constructed. The research institutions creating conscious minds in their simulations may be required by law to place their creations in Chip Haven, but they will probably want to spend as little money as possible doing so. The organization managing our afterlife may try to make it as pleasant as possible, all while facing constant budget constraints. Like a chimpanzee sanctuary with walls and fake trees, our afterlife may be surprisingly small and full of obvious glitches.

The possibility of glitches raises an important question: Will we be told we are in a simulated afterlife? Any obvious bugs would certainly make it difficult to keep the minds stuck in Chip Haven from realizing they are in a simulation. To forestall such a shocking realization, perhaps every new consciousness added to Chip Haven will receive a tutorial explaining that they are only simulated beings. While we are experiments in a simulated world, scientists would use every trick available to keep us from realizing we are in a model, as such a realization would skew the results of the experiment. After we have played our part in the model and died, though, there remains no reason to keep our true origin a secret. Additionally, it would be unethical to continue to hide our true natures, as keeping such information from us when it is no longer necessary to do so would be cruel. After our death in the model, we will likely be informed that we are simulated beings, and that our reward for involuntary participation in a science experiment is a simulated heaven.

Besides wondering about the design of Chip Haven, we must also consider how long our simulated afterlife will last. When we think about life after death, we usually assume that the afterlife will persist for eternity. Eternity is a pretty long time, though. As far as we know, everything, including the universe itself, eventually ends. No logical reason exists to assume that the afterlife won't also have an expiration date. Just as life ends in death, life after death may also end in death.

In considering how long our simulated afterlife may last, we can begin by making the assumption that the computers running the simulation will be on the physical Earth (it seems unlikely a future civilization would consider Chip Haven important enough to be placed somewhere safer). In approximately 3.5 billion years, the sun will increase in brightness enough that liquid water on Earth will completely evaporate. With the vaporization of liquid water, life will be impossible, and the planet will become completely barren. While unlikely, perhaps a computer or two might survive, still happily running a simulated afterlife. In about 5 billion years, though, the sun will become a red giant, growing large enough to devour Mercury, Venus, and finally Earth. No computer, no matter how intent on running its programming, would survive Earth being obliterated by the sun. Admittedly, the idea that a computer program could keep running for 5 billion years approaches absurdity, but at least it puts an upper limit on the afterlife.

Five billion years on the physical Earth may be the absolute limit for a computer simulating the afterlife, but we have no reason to believe that a year in the simulation takes a year on Earth. In fact, that would be extremely unlikely. A scientist running a model of humanity would not want to wait around an entire year just for a year to pass in her model. In the future it may be possible to run a full simulation, accounting for billions of human minds spanning 350,000 years of human history, during a single afternoon. Similarly, a simulated afterlife could seem to stretch for billions upon billions of years for the minds within the computer, while only taking a couple of decades in the physical world.

Returning to the chimpanzees in their sanctuaries — the research institutions that paid for the apes to be housed in those sanctuaries did so with the understanding that the chimpanzees would eventually die, and there would at some point be no more need to pay for their upkeep. Quite possibly a similar deal would exist for any simulated humans housed in a simulated afterlife. A future civilization may find it perfectly reasonable to terminate our simulated afterlife after an acceptably lengthy expanse of time. Would that be a billion years, a million years, maybe only a thousand? Impossible to guess. But certainly not impossible to assume that any research institution on the financial hook for funding an afterlife would negotiate a finite amount of time that it would have to pay for it.

From all this we may conclude that our simulated afterlife won't last for eternity, but it will probably last for a really, really long time. Maybe not a long time in the physical world, but certainly a long time in the world of the simulation. A billion years in paradise may not be as great a reward as an eternity in paradise, but it should at least be enough time to catch up on all those television shows you missed while you were alive. On the other hand, if the contractor running Chip Haven has to cut a few corners in its digital construction, then a billion years in paradise may end up being more than enough time!

Maybe A Bit Too Negative

In hindsight, the last section seems overly pessimistic. After all, if you die and find out that you get to live billions of years in an afterlife with no pain, disease, or hunger, that sounds like a pretty amazing reward. The afterlife that has been constructed for us may not be perfect, but an imperfect paradise is better than no paradise at all.

More importantly, there is a reason to believe that our simulated minds will receive better treatment than the chimpanzees. While most of us respect the cognitive abilities of the great apes, we still view apes as having a level of consciousness less than that of humans. If we are human minds created in a computer by living humans to simulate the humans that came before, then our creators would almost certainly see in us a clear reflection of themselves. Seeing themselves in us, hopefully the scientists who created us would want to give us the best version of the afterlife possible.

Wondering about the motivation and reasoning of our creators, though, raises an important question: What can we safely assume about the beings who made us?

What Do We Know About Our Creators?

So far in this chapter, I have assumed that the physical humans in the future experimenting on us are basically the same as we are. That means I am presupposing that a future civilization has a similar set of values and morals as our own—that people in the future share our belief in the importance of love and compassion, and respect for other conscious minds. We need to be careful, though, because that's nearly the same assumption theologians make about God.

Traditional religions teach that God rewards His creations with an afterlife because God consists of a perfect and all-encompassing love and compassion. Why does God have perfect love and compassion? Most likely because humans value love and compassion, and we assume God must be a perfect bundle of all the things we value (and sullied by none of the things we despise). Humans value consciousness, therefore, God must value consciousness to such a profound degree that He constructs an afterlife so that humans may enjoy their consciousness for eternity.

Of course, the obvious problem in a belief that God contains nothing but perfect goodness arises from the observation that if a God exists, He must constantly consent to bad things happening. Many religious philosophers argue that God allows evil to occur because God created humans with free will to allow us to make our own choices—and making evil choices just happens to be something humans are particularly good at.

This highlights the problem with assuming that the physical humans in the future are just like us. Why would humans from a future civilization who presumably value love and compassion allow bad things to happen in the simulated worlds they create?

We might assume that horrible things happen in our world because the scientists must allow those things to happen to test their predictions of human behavior. Perhaps we can even rationalize suffering the occasional horrible occurrence if it means we are rewarded with an afterlife that lasts millions or billions of simulated years.

But what if we are completely wrong about our creators? What if they share none of our values and morals? In fact, we can again invoke basic probability to suggest that the physical humans running our simulation are very different from us.

As explained earlier in the chapter, a scientist running a simulation varies the parameters of the model to figure out how changing those parameters changes the outcome of the simulation. For instance, in a simulation of human behavior, one of the parameters may be the level of altruism the average human displays toward strangers. There will be some runs of the model where humans are very altruistic, willing to literally give the shirts off their backs to a fellow human in need. Conversely, there will be some runs where the average human would never even consider helping a stranger, maybe even believing that helping a stranger is immoral.

The physical humans running the model will have a certain level of average altruism in their society. The models they run, though, will use a wide range of altruism levels. The same will be true for all the other parameters in the model—there will be one value for the physical humans, but a range of values for use in the models. This means that there will be millions of simulations with parameters different from the physical world, and many fewer simulations with parameters exactly the same as the physical world. For any simulation we happen to find ourselves in, most likely the parameters that make up our world will be different from the parameters in the physical world. The level of altruism humans display in a particular simulation will probably be different from the level displayed by their physical creators.

Perhaps I'm naïve, but I like to believe that most people place a great deal of importance on protecting other human life and respecting all human consciousness. We don't really know, though, whether the physical humans that created us share those same values. Quite possibly the simulation we find ourselves in has the parameters for protecting human life and respecting human consciousness at extremely high levels. The physical humans that created our simulation, on the other hand, may care very little about any consciousness other than their own, and may see no need or value in protecting or rewarding any human minds they create as science experiments.

The result of all this potential fiddling with parameters is that it ultimately threatens the possibility of the afterlife. If the physical humans that created our simulation have morals very different from our own, they may see no reason to reward us with life after simulated death.

But once again, I seem to revel a bit too much in the potential negatives. While it is possible that our creators do not share our respect for human life, it is equally likely that they value human life and human consciousness much more than we do. We may happen to find ourselves in a simulation where the parameters for altruism, respect for other humans, and reverence for consciousness exist at levels much lower than the levels in the physical world. The scientists who created us may hold a near reverence for every conscious mind they create, and may put just as much effort into rewarding those minds for helping to advance scientific inquiry as they spend in the actual simulation of the world.

If we do happen to find ourselves in a simulation where people treat each other more cruelly than physical humans do, then the life awaiting us after we die may be particularly grand. The scientists may respect consciousness so much that creating human minds and placing them in paradise exists as nearly the entire point of the simulation. Consider the Tamagotchi from the beginning of the chapter. Millions of people bought the toy simply to have a digital creature to look after. If the owners of the Tamagotchi toys could have given their pets a digital afterlife, I bet nearly every single one would have done so.

Alright, But What Do We *Really* Know About Our Creators?

The little aliens born in the Tamagotchis may represent an even better analogy to our current existence than first seems likely. No creatures resembling the Tamagotchi aliens have ever existed in the world. The alien creatures were invented for the toy because they seemed more fun, and easier to simulate, than digital humans. The exact same reasoning may explain why we were created.

Perhaps no physical human designed our simulated minds; instead, an alien species that looks, thinks, and acts completely different from us may be our creators. Arising out of scientific inquiry, or just for fun, our alien programmers may have decided to simulate a creature that has never existed before. After throwing together some gangly limbs, a distinct lack of fur, and a bizarre fondness for eating oysters, they ended up with humans. We must consider the possibility that no human being has ever existed in the physical universe.

If we have been simulated by an alien species, then we return to the problem that we had before—we know very little about the values and morals of the beings who created us. The alien scientists running our simulation may not care about any lives but their own, or any conscious minds but their own. The aliens may attach very little significance to the made-up creatures they have brought into existence.

On the other hand, the aliens who created us may care about us more than we seem to care about ourselves. In fact, such a possible reality may be the more likely outcome. The reason has to do with the types of societies that would eventually become advanced enough to be able to simulate conscious minds.

To form a complex society, any species—whether alien or human—must have a certain basic respect for others. A species consisting of nothing but individuals who care only about themselves would not be able to work together well enough to create a complex society. Certainly, they would not work together well enough to advance scientific understanding far enough to create simulated consciousness. As a result, we may reasonably hope that any physical beings that created us would value the conscious minds they have created, and would want to give those minds an afterlife of genuine pleasure and joy.

The Morality Of A Simulated Afterlife

If we truly are simulations, the above arguments suggest that our creators value us enough to give us an enjoyable afterlife. But the existence of such an afterlife doesn't eliminate some rather vexing questions about the presence of good and evil in this pre-afterlife world.

If we are part of an experiment meant to test how human minds react to different situations, then is anything we do truly good or evil? Can we be held responsible for our actions if our actions are being manipulated by a scientist conducting an experiment? This concern about morality becomes even more pressing if we happen to find ourselves in a simulation where the scientists have changed the parameters to make humans particularly selfish or spiteful. If the researchers tweaked the parameters to make it more probable that the simulated humans will act in greedy or malicious ways, then when people perform greedy or malicious acts are they at fault for simply following their programming? Conversely, are your actions good and noble if the parameters set at the beginning of the model made it more probable that you would perform good and noble acts? In other words, can we weigh any action as truly good or evil if someone puts a thumb on the scale?

Unfortunately, I don't think satisfactory answers to these questions exist. How much credit we deserve for our actions, and how much credit belongs to the computer program (or society, or family, or genes) that shaped us, is a question that has bedeviled philosophers for centuries.

Simulated Life After Death

This world sure seems real, but maybe we're programmed to be amazed at just how real everything seems. While we all like to believe that our minds are unique—brilliant compositions vibrating with a symphony of beautiful thoughts—the truth may be much more mundane. Nothing you can think is so unique that a computer will not eventually be able to think it for you. This means that someday scientists will almost certainly be able to simulate human consciousness within a computer. Chances are those scientists will simulate many billions more conscious minds than have ever existed in the physical world.

Probability says we are more likely to be simulated beings than physical ones.

This may seem rather depressing at first—who could possibly prefer being a computer program to being a real, living human? But the upsides to being a simulation are immense. Whoever created us will most likely feel morally responsible (or at least legally responsible) to reward us with a paradise that lasts for millions, if not billions, of years. Turns out, being stuck in a computer might be pretty awesome.

CHAPTER 3

BLOCK UNIVERSE

When you were an infant, about three months old, something remarkable happened in your still-developing brain—you began to realize that even if you couldn't see or touch an object, that didn't mean the object no longer existed. All infants go through this developmental milestone, beginning to understand that physical objects do not simply disappear when they can no longer be seen. Psychologists call this phenomenon object permanence.

As adults we have no trouble believing that an object a hundred miles away exists, even if we can't see or touch it. When a relative who lives in a different city calls you on the phone, you're not surprised because you know that people and objects that are physically distant from you still exist. Object permanence forms such a basic foundation for our understanding of the universe that after about three month of age we take it completely for granted.

Interestingly, we have no corresponding understanding of temporal permanence. We believe that the present moment in time is real, but that the past has already occurred and cannot be changed, and that the future has yet to occur but can never be reached. Deep in our bones we believe that only the thinnest slice of time truly exists. We intuitively believe that because we cannot see and touch the past or the present that they must not exist.

We are, however, almost certainly wrong. Several of the greatest scientific discoveries of the twentieth century show that our intuitive understanding of how time behaves is completely mistaken. We are like babies whose brains have not yet developed enough for us to grasp that even though we cannot see them or touch them, the past and the future both still exist.

The Flow Of Time

For thousands of years of human history, only mystics, opium users, and philosophers who happened to be opium users questioned whether time traveled in one direction—from the past to the present to the future. For almost every person who has ever lived, there has been no need to question the nature of time, as every instinct tells us that time flows one way. We seem to have no choice but to be carried along for the ride.

This understanding of time changed abruptly, however, when Albert Einstein proposed his special and general theories of relativity. Time no longer flowed inexorably in one direction—it took detours through backwaters, passed through branching deltas, and formed the occasional whirlpool. I'm afraid the arguments in this chapter require a brief explanation of the special and general theories of relativity. If you're not particularly fond of theoretic physics, no need to worry—I won't be describing the theories in detail. Instead, the following sections will highlight the more important points that deal with the surprising characteristics of time. If you are interested in reading more about the special and general theories of relativity, though, it's hard to beat Einstein explaining the theories himself in *Relativity: The Special and the General Theory*.

The following explanations of our current understanding of time point to the most scientifically accepted view by which life after death exists. In fact, the version of life after death described in this chapter appears to be the version that Einstein himself believed in.

Special Relativity

Albert Einstein described the theory that became known as special relativity in a scientific paper published in 1905. The concept was later given the name "special" because it assumes gravity is not present, thereby making it a special case. Einstein, always hoping to explain as much of the universe as possible, took care of gravity later in what would become his general theory of relativity.

Beginning with the special theory of relativity, Einstein based the entire notion on two simple ideas: 1) the laws of physics are the same in all non-accelerating frames of reference; and 2) the speed of light in a vacuum is a constant and the same for all observers. Alright, these two "simple" ideas aren't so simple at all. The important thing to understand is that if these two ideas are both correct, then time may seem to flow differently for different observers.

A simple way to visualize this comes from a thought experiment. Imagine a beam of light bouncing between two mirrors.[3] Light travels at 186,300 miles per second, so if we set the first mirror on the floor and the second mirror 93,150 miles above it, a beam of light traveling from the first mirror on the floor, bouncing off the second mirror on the ceiling, and returning to the first mirror, would take exactly one second. We could use this device as a clock, counting the number of times the beam of light returns to the mirror on the floor as the passing of each second.

Now imagine we put this unconventional light clock on a spaceship (admittedly, one of the larger class of spaceships that happens to be 93,150 miles tall). We decide we want to take our clock for a trip, so we accelerate our spaceship to half the speed of light. For those of us on the spaceship, the clock seems to be working perfectly fine, the light bouncing between the two mirrors, counting off each new second. However, for any observer who happens to be sitting still, watching our spaceship go by, something strange would seem to be happening.

Inside the spaceship the light would be bouncing straight up and down between the two mirrors. To the observer outside the spaceship, though, the motion of the spaceship would make the light appear to trace out a zig-zag line as it bounces between the mirrors. Figure 3 shows what the light clock would look like to those of us in the spaceship, as well as what it would look like to the stationary observer.

This presents an enormous problem. For us in the spaceship, the light appears to be going straight up and down, covering 186,300 miles every second. To the stationary observer though, the light isn't going straight up and down at all—the observer clearly sees the light tracing out a zig-zag pattern. For the observer, when the light travels from the mirror on the floor to the mirror on the ceiling, and then back to the floor, it appears to travel 208,290 miles. Does that mean that to the stationary observer light travels at 208,290 miles per second? Absolutely not! Nothing, not even light, can travel faster than 186,300 miles per second.

To get out of this conundrum, we are forced to conclude that time itself changes. To the stationary observer, light must still travel 186,300 miles per second as it traces out the zig-zag pattern. This means that for the observer, time on the spaceship appears to be moving slower than the observer's own time. To the observer, time on the spaceship would appear to slow down by about 10 percent. If the stationary observer used his own clock, he would find that the light takes 1.1 seconds to bounce between the mirrors. If the spaceship were going even faster, the light would trace

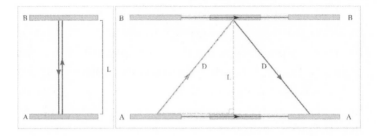

Figure 3. A light clock formed by a pulse of light bouncing between mirrors A and B. The left panel shows what the light clock looks like to someone on a spaceship carrying the clock. A pulse of light travels from mirror A on the floor of the spaceship up to mirror B, covering distance L. The light then bounces off mirror B and travels back to mirror A. To the person on the spaceship, the light appears to be moving straight up and down. The right panel shows what the light clock looks like to a stationary observer. As the spaceship flies by, the light appears to trace out the zig-zag line D. The segments of line D are longer than L, so it would seem that the light travels both distance L and distance D in the same amount of time. This cannot occur, though, as the light travels at a constant velocity. To overcome this paradox, time on the spaceship must be moving slower relative to the stationary observer's time. Sacamol, CC BY-SA.

out an even more elongated zig-zag pattern, meaning that to the observer, time on the spaceship would seem to be going even slower. If it were possible for the spaceship to move at the speed of light, time aboard the ship would appear to stop.

This time dilation goes for everything on the spaceship, including us as we take the ship out for a spin. Because we are moving at half the speed of light, we would be aging 10 percent slower than the stationary observer. We wouldn't notice anything different, though, as we sped around in our rocket—the light would continue to take exactly one second to bounce between the mirrors, and we would seem to age at a normal rate. It would only be when we finished cruising around and stopped to have a chat with the stationary observer that we would see that we had aged much slower than he had.

This thought experiment demonstrates that time is not the constant, unvarying ruler of our lives we instinctively believe it to be. Of course, one could simply argue that a thought experiment proves nothing, and time remains as unvarying as ever. Scientific experiment after scientific experiment, however, have confirmed the special theory of relativity and the inconsistent nature of time. For example, atomic clocks flown on airplanes record less time passing relative to stationary clocks on the ground. In fact, special relativity must be taken into consideration when making sure that the clocks on satellites orbiting at high speeds around Earth do not become unsynchronized from stationary clocks on Earth. Through special relativity and the experiments that confirm it, we have come to understand that time does not exist as some separate measure of the universe, distinct from space. In fact, the three dimensions of space and the one dimension of time are not separate entities—they are fused together to form the four dimensions called space-time. Perhaps object permanence and temporal permanence have more in common than first seems possible.

Beyond showing how time changes with motion, the theory of special relativity also proved that the order in which events occur may not always be fixed. This can be understood with another thought experiment.

Imagine a train moving quickly down a set of railroad tracks. One person sits on board, in the very center of the train; meanwhile, a second person stands still on a platform, watching as the train speeds by. Just as the person on the train and the person on the platform pass each other, a lightning bolt strikes at the exact center of the train.

For the person on the train (who miraculously avoided being struck by the lightning), the flash of light given off by the lightning bolt is equally distant from the front and back of the train. As a result, light from the lightning bolt will reach the front and back of the train at the exact same moment. The person on the platform, however, will see something very different.

For the person on the platform, the front of the train is quickly moving away from the flash of light from the lightning bolt, while the back of the train is quickly moving toward the flash of light. To the person on the platform, the light will clearly reach the back of the train before it reaches the front of the train. These two individuals, one on the train and one on the platform, will report very different observations about when the light from the lightning bolt reached the two ends of the train. Which observer is correct? They are both correct, and in admitting that they are both correct, we again must admit that our intuitive understanding of time does not match reality. Even the order in time in which events occur may change from one person to the next.

General Relativity

After elucidating the theory of special relativity, Einstein wanted to determine how gravity would influence the framework he had developed. In 1915, Einstein proposed what would become known as the general theory of relativity. General relativity takes the insights of special relativity and applies them to gravity. Just as movement changes our understanding of time, so does gravity.

General relativity states that the stronger the gravitational field experienced by a clock, the slower time passes for that clock. Compare two people, one standing on Bourbon Street in New Orleans, while the other stands on top of Mount Everest. The person in New Orleans, being closer to the core of the earth, experiences a stronger gravitational field than the person on Mount Everest, who stands farther away from the center of the earth. For the person standing in New Orleans, time passes very slightly slower than for the person standing at the top of Mount Everest (although if it's Mardi Gras in New Orleans and blizzarding in the Himalayas, I make no claims about the seeming movement of time).

The difference in the passage of time for a person in New Orleans versus one on Mount Everest would be very small. In fact, Earth's core has experienced stronger gravity than the surface for billions of years, but is only about 2.5 years younger. This small difference in the ticking of time close to Earth versus farther away must again be taken into consideration for satellites orbiting the planet, however. The clocks on satellites in orbit around the planet must be corrected not only for their velocity relative to stationary clocks on Earth, but also for the difference in gravitational field.

While the relative change in the movement of time in New Orleans compared to Mount Everest may be small, when gravity becomes stronger, it has a much greater effect. The objects with the strongest gravitational fields in the universe are black holes. In fact, black holes have such strong gravitational fields that nothing can escape from them, not even light. Scientists call the threshold surrounding a black hole, from which nothing can escape, the event horizon. If we decided to take our special relativity spaceship for another flight, but accidentally flew too close to a black hole and reached the event horizon, the gravitational field would be immense. To an outside observer, it would appear as though time had completely stopped on our spaceship.

One Big Block

Thousands of experiments have confirmed the predictions of special and general relativity. Although it seems contrary to our deepest intuition, time does not behave as a continuous, never-varying current tugging the universe ever forward. Time flows relatively faster or slower depending on where you are, how fast you're moving, and who you happen to be watching speed by.

More importantly, as Einstein so elegantly proved, space and time are not separate measures of the universe—they are intertwined with each other to form space-time. Just as we accept that objects distant from us in space exist even though we cannot see or touch them, the behavior of time suggests that objects distant from us in time also exist even though we cannot see or touch them. Just as all of space, throughout the entire universe, exists together simultaneously, perhaps all of time, throughout eternity, also exists together simultaneously.

Physicists call the idea that every moment in time exists together simultaneously the block universe hypothesis. They call it a block universe because the entirety of space and time—past, present, and future—exists, forever and unchanging, as one big four-dimensional space-time block. Occasionally you may see the block universe hypothesis referred to as eternalism, in that every moment in time exists for eternity. Conversely, the idea that only the present moment exists usually gets labeled as presentism.

Hopefully, my discussion of the special and general theories of relativity has convinced you that presentism does a horrible job of explaining the universe. If time moves more slowly with speed or gravity, and if the order in which events occur depends on who happens to be observing them, then what exactly do we mean by "the present?"

Fortunately, the block universe hypothesis does a much better job of accounting for the vagaries of time. In the block universe hypothesis, we do not need to assume that all observers are present in the exact same moment—if all moments exist simultaneously, then my present moment does not need to be the same as your present moment. Under the block universe hypothesis, no transcendental metronome exists to beat out the rhythm of time, and therefore we have no need for every present moment to align.

Memories Of The Future

The block universe hypothesis has many adherents among working physicists (although, to be fair, many other physicists believe in a strict version of presentism). The block universe hypothesis certainly seems to have the advantage of explaining the special and general theories of relativity more coherently than presentism. The biggest objection to the hypothesis, though, arises from a simple question: If both the past and the future exist simultaneously with the present, why can we remember the past but we can't remember the future? In other words, if every moment of time—past, present, and future—exists at the same time, why do we only experience the present and only remember the past?

To try to answer this question, we can begin by exploring why we consciously experience only the present moment. In the block universe hypothesis, every moment in time truly is the present for the conscious mind in that moment. Every moment in time may exist simultaneously, but at each moment in time your conscious mind only experiences that moment as the present moment. Put another way, you exist as a conscious being in the moment you are reading this sentence, while at the same time you also exist as a conscious being in the moment before you began reading the sentence and in the moment after you have finished reading the sentence. Through every moment in the block universe in which you are conscious, you are experiencing the present moment. Each of those moments exists as the present for your conscious mind for all eternity.

This may explain why we consciously experience the present, but not the past or the future, but it does not answer why we can remember the past but not the future. There must be some reason why it intuitively feels as though time flows from the past to the future, but never in the other direction. Unfortunately, there are no entirely satisfactory answers. The most likely explanation springs from the way in which the universe began. We may have the big bang to blame for why time seems to flow in only one direction.

The theory of the big bang holds that during the beginning of the universe, the matter in the universe was very evenly distributed. Importantly, this even distribution of matter resulted in the early universe being in a state of very low entropy. I discuss entropy in more detail in Chapter 9, so I will only give a brief description here.

As you may recall from a high school chemistry class, entropy measures the disorder of a system. The second law of thermodynamics states that the entropy of a closed system never decreases over time; in other words, over time systems become more random.

For example, if you happen to find yourself in a classroom teaching approximately twenty undergraduate students about mitosis, and you happen to pass gas, it would be extremely unlikely for those gas molecules to stay bunched up in a corner of the classroom. Instead, the second law of thermodynamics predicts that the molecules will randomly spread throughout the classroom, increasing the entropy of the system, and producing several extremely embarrassing giggles.

The observant reader will have noticed that according to the second law of thermodynamics, entropy increases *over time*. This reliance on the direction of time is actually very rare in physics. Most physics equations work equally well going forward or backward in time (which in itself should strengthen our belief that time does not behave as the one-way road we instinctively think it to be). Entropy, though, does increase in only one direction. When considering the definition of entropy, what exactly does *over time* mean in the context of a block universe?

In the initial moments of the big bang, all the matter in the universe was condensed in a uniform state of very low entropy. In an admittedly rather juvenile analogy, the big bang is like the moment when someone has just passed gas in a classroom and the gas has yet to spread randomly around the room. As the low-entropy matter from the early seconds of the big bang began to spread and form into the clumps that would eventually become galaxies and planets and people, the entropy of the universe increased.

This increase in entropy, from the initial moments of the big bang to the present, may explain why time in the block universe seems to flow in one direction. Imagine yourself looking at the block universe from above, as one gigantic mass of space and time. At one end of the block the big bang occurs, beginning the block in a state of low entropy. As your eyes scan across the block, you notice the entropy within the block increasing — like watching a bit of red dye dropped onto the top of a glass of still water, the dye spreading out as it sinks to the bottom of the glass. Similarly, because of the big bang starting the universe in a state of low entropy, the entropy in the block universe increases in only one direction. For this reason, we perceive time as flowing in one direction in the block universe. The increase in entropy caused by the initial state of the big bang results in our remembering the past, but not the future, even though the past, present, and future all exist within the block universe simultaneously. Our intuitive belief that time only flows in one direction is merely an illusion, brought about simply by the block universe beginning in such a peculiar state. You may not be able to remember the future, but the future you that already exists in the block universe remembers you.

A Growing Block

While the low entropy of the big bang may explain why we cannot remember the future, physicists have proposed another plausible hypothesis. Perhaps we cannot remember the future because the block universe is growing, continually adding new moments to the block.

In the growing block universe hypothesis, the past and the present exist simultaneously, just as in the regular block universe hypothesis. In a growing block universe, though, the future does not yet exist. As the present moment moves forward, overtaking the future and becoming the past, the growing block universe adds another slice to the block of space-time. Under this hypothesis, the growing block universe began as an infinitely thin block at the first moment of the big bang, and has been getting larger with each passing second since then.

The growing block universe seems to fit better with our intuitive understanding of the flow of time—that the past and present are real, but the future does not yet exist. One problem with the growing block universe hypothesis, though, arises from the way in which it privileges the growing edge of the block. Does the growing edge of the block represent the "real" present moment while every other moment in the block are not similarly as real? Why should we expect one part of the block universe to be more real than any other?

Although this does seem to be a problem with the growing block universe hypothesis, it may also present the solution for why we intuitively believe only the present moment to exist. In the growing block universe, the growing edge of the block is indeed special. At that growing edge, our conscious mind somehow feels that the present moment is special, and we cannot remember the future because the future does not exist yet. This feeling of the present being special gets recorded in our minds as the growing block universe expands. Further back in the block universe, well behind the growing edge, our conscious mind still exists in every previous moment. However, as each slice was added to the block, we felt the present to be special at that moment, and so for eternity we will continue to feel that each moment in the block is the present moment, and that we can remember the past but not the future.

The Block Universe And The Afterlife

The way in which a block universe forms, and the consequences for our experience of the present moment, are certainly interesting. More important to this book, though, is figuring out what the block universe hypothesis tell us about the possibility of the afterlife.

In a block universe, every moment throughout eternity exists simultaneously, so there can be no such thing as "after." There is no period of time after your death if every moment in time exists simultaneously. Being within a block universe means that each second of your life exists forever. This obviously also means that your conscious mind exists forever. There may be sections where your conscious mind is not present—sections where you are not yet born or sections where you have died—but the moments where you are alive and where your conscious mind exists will always be there.

The concept of the afterlife promises that your mind will exist for eternity. The block universe hypothesis states with absolute certainty that your mind will exist for eternity, and that you are alive forever. By every definition of the word, you are immortal.

You're probably mumbling at the pages of this book right now, pointing out that if there are sections of the block universe that extend past the point at which you died, then life after death does not really exist. If you die, and your life ceases after you have died, then there is no afterlife.

As I already argued, though, in a block universe the idea of "before" and "after" are meaningless. There are sections of the block in which you exist, and sections of the block in which you don't exist, but in the sections of the block in which you do exist, you exist for all eternity. For many people, one of the great regrets in facing death comes from the fear that all the memories accumulated over a lifetime will be completely lost. In a block universe, not only do your memories continue to exist forever, the very moments in which those memories were formed continue to exist forever. The idea of the afterlife holds little meaning when life and death coexist for eternity.

While it may not be a well-known concept, the block universe hypothesis is not at all a fringe idea—many physicists believe that the best way of explaining the oddities of time comes from understanding our universe as a giant block of space-time. In fact, Einstein himself appears to have believed in the block universe hypothesis. His understanding of the block universe also seems to have led him to conclude that when we die, we do not truly cease to exist. This can be seen most clearly in a letter Einstein wrote in 1955.

Michele Besso was an engineer and a close friend of Einstein when they were students at the Federal Polytechnic Institute in Zurich. In 1955, Besso died at the age of eighty-one, and Einstein composed a letter of condolence to Besso's family. In the letter, Einstein wrote, "Now he has departed from this strange world a little ahead of me. That means nothing. For us believing physicists the distinction between past, present, and future only has the meaning of an illusion, though a persistent one."

Regardless of whether the universe turns out to be a block universe or a growing block universe, the result for life after death will be the same: your conscious mind will continue to exist within the block throughout all eternity. While still scary, your death remains but one moment in the universe, and does nothing to erase your existence throughout the rest of the block. We are all immortal because time does not erase the past, time simply catalogues it.

Consequences Of A Block Universe

Just as Chapter 2 pointed out that there may be some unintended consequences to an advanced civilization simulating our minds, a block universe may also have some rather unpalatable consequences. Let's start by assuming that we find ourselves in a regular block universe, not a growing block universe. If so, then the past, present, and future all exist simultaneously. To rephrase the previous sentence to place the emphasis where it needs to be—in a block universe, the future already exists!

The future already existing has some rather dire ramifications. In a regular block universe, any decision you make, you have already made. The script for the rest of your life has already been written and acted out. Nothing you do will be able to change the future course of your life. Does the block universe hypothesis mean that none of us have free will? The question of whether we do or do not have free will is of course one of the fundamental debates raging across all of philosophy. Against my better judgment, I dip a toe into this debate in Chapter 8. For now, let me just suggest that a seeming lack of free will does not portend the lack of personal agency it seems to imply—your future may already exist, but that does not mean it was any hand but your own that wrote it.

Instead of worrying about free will, let's instead turn to another consequence of the block universe: If every moment in time exists forever, then you are consciously experiencing every moment in your life forever. Every single moment of your life will be one you live in for eternity.

The upside of this is that throughout all eternity, you are consciously experiencing the very best moments of your life. Right now, the most amazing, most exciting, most peaceful moments of your life are not a mere memory—you are consciously experiencing each and every one of them. This, of course, has a very serious downside as well—you are also consciously experiencing the very worst moments of your life for all eternity as well. Each heartbreak, each moment of physical and emotional pain, will be consciously experienced forever.

Realizing that you will continue to experience all the moments of your life for eternity imposes a rather heavy psychological burden. You've likely heard the aphorism, "live each day as if it were your last." The idea is that you should try to make every day of your life meaningful, or at least enjoyable, because you never know if that day might be your last day. This seems woefully inadequate, though, in a block universe. How should you live your life if you will be experiencing each moment forever? Your feeling of boredom as you stand in line at the grocery store will exist forever. The pain you feel when you stub your toe will exist for all eternity. As a duty to your conscious self, shouldn't you try to make each and every moment of your life as joyous as possible, because some version of you will be stuck in that moment forever?

Unfortunately, experiencing nothing but pure joy throughout every second of every day is completely impossible. The very process of staying alive means that there will be moments spent sleeping, going to the bathroom, and eating bowls of cereal over the sink. Despite our best intentions, the very process of living means that some of the moments in our lives will have to contain boredom or fear or sadness. As a consequence, each of us must sacrifice some of the moments in our lives to unhappiness and boredom so that other moments may contain joy and peacefulness.

While it would be nice if every moment of our lives could be truly joyous, perhaps the knowledge that we will have moments of pain and drudgery that exist for eternity may provide a certain clarity to our existence. When we are trapped in a moment of boredom or sadness, it may help us to feel better about that moment to realize that we are sacrificing now so that we may experience other moments of joy for eternity. Conversely, when we are feeling moments of joy or peacefulness, we should try to remind ourselves that while we are lucky to experience those moments forever, they could not have occurred without other versions of ourselves in other moments sacrificing their own happiness.

When balancing joyous moments with sad, the difficult part comes in trying to get the ratio right. Hopefully, throughout your existence in the block universe, the moments of happiness are more numerous than the moments of sadness.

Block Universe Afterlife

As Einstein understood, the special and general theories of relativity did more than upend our understanding of time—they also upended our understanding of life and death. If your conscious mind exists for all eternity, in what way does death even matter? There may be some parts of the block universe in which you don't exist, but the parts of the block universe in which you do exist are there forever. There is nothing that any human or god can do to erase your conscious mind from eternity. The afterlife truly exists because every moment of your life is its own afterlife.

CHAPTER 4

THE ENTANGLED LIFE

As the best ghost stories tend to do, this one begins with a person traveling alone on a deserted country road. The person, Sir William Napier, was riding his horse from Bedfordshire, England, to the nearby county of Berkshire. He had started the journey early that morning, but now the sun was beginning to sink below the trees, causing the shadows to grow long.

Realizing that he would soon need to stop for the night, Sir William rounded a bend in the road and found himself in front of a small inn. The inn was well kept, with the masonry in front recently whitewashed. However, it was situated behind several large trees in such a way that a traveler could find it only by accident.

Knocking on the front door, Sir William was pleased to find that there was one room left for rent. Being shown upstairs to his room by the maid, the candles that had already been lit allowed him to discern that the room was agreeably large, and decorated in a manner only slightly below what a man of his station was accustomed to.

The bed had been placed in the center of the room and had a frame of stained wood forming a canopy from which thick purple cloth hung, hiding the mattress. Feeling tired and ready for sleep, Sir William pulled back the fabric shrouding the bed. Lying motionless in the bed was a corpse.

Sir William let out a yelp and took several steps back, letting the cloth again hide the mattress. After several seconds Sir William regained his fortitude, and he approached the bed again, pulling back the canopy. The green skin of the corpse, beginning to bloat, betrayed that the body had died several days before.

From his clothing, Sir William could tell that the corpse was clearly that of a gentleman. Amazingly, the dead man appeared to have on almost the exact same riding outfit that Sir William himself wore. Looking more closely at the face of the corpse, Sir William felt a shiver of recognition. Although the skin was distorted, he could tell that the face of the corpse was his own face. The dead man lying in the bed was him.

Sir William ran to the door of his room and called loudly for the owner of the inn, wanting to know what kind of malicious jest was being had at his expense. When the innkeeper and his wife arrived in the room, they moved the cloth surrounding the bed to find no hint of a corpse. Indeed, the sheets of the bed had not even been rumpled—they lay perfectly undisturbed, just as the maid had placed them there that morning.

Not sure whether he had experienced a hallucination brought on by the weariness of travel or whether he truly was the victim of a prank, Sir William quickly left the inn. He slept that night several miles up the road beneath an oak tree.

Eventually, Sir William's journey ended, and he reached Berkshire. By nightfall, though, he had developed a fever, and within a fortnight the brave traveler was dead.

Traveling back along the road by which it had come, Sir William's body took several days to return to Bedfordshire. When the family opened his casket they could barely recognize the corpse looking back at them, as its features were so skewed by green, bloated skin. The body they stared at looked exactly like the one Sir William had found in his bed at the inn.

Now of course this is simply a silly ghost story, taken from *Haunted England: A Survey of English Ghost-Lore*, by Christina Hole. Several cultures have folk stories of people who have seen ghostly versions of themselves. In this telling of the story, Sir William saw a *fetch*—an apparition exactly replicating a particular person. According to Irish folklore, seeing your *fetch* in the morning meant good luck, while seeing your *fetch* after nightfall meant that your death was near.

With all due respect to Sir William, the idea that there exists a version of you in a different plane of reality seems outlandish. As this chapter suggests, though, the possibility of something similar to a *fetch* may be more likely than it first appears. The previous chapter discussed how to an outside observer, motion and gravity can cause time to appear to slow down. That motion and gravity can influence time seems amazing, but in the previous chapter we only scratched the surface of just how astonishing the universe may be. At the quantum level of the universe—the level of the atomic scale—particles that are vast distances from each other seem to communicate with each other faster than the speed of light, energy appears in completely empty space, and the universe we find ourselves in may be only one of trillions of similar universes.

This chapter considers two ways in which the quantum world may allow life after death: The multiverse and the quantum mind. Both these possible routes to the afterlife rely on the strange, nonintuitive nature of the quantum world. For that reason, I begin with a bit of background on the quantum level of nature.

Collapsing Waves

When most of us think of an electron, we think of a tiny little ball, whizzing in a circle around the nucleus of an atom. Our concept of what an electron looks like comes from years of staring at illustrations of atoms in schoolbooks. In the standard interpretation of the quantum world, however, the electron as a discrete particle doesn't exist—or at least the electron particle doesn't exist until we decide to observe whether it exists or not. Instead, before we observe them, quantum particles exist as wave functions.

A wave function provides the probabilities of where in space a particle can be. In other words, before we observe it, the electron more closely resembles a cloud. When we observe the electron, we may be more likely to find it in one part of the cloud than another, but until we do observe it the electron could be at any point in that cloud.

You might reasonably think that the wave function provides the probabilities for where the electron may be located, but that the electron actually exists as a discrete particle in one definite location within the cloud—we're just not sure where until we measure it. While this may seem reasonable, decades of physics experiments show it to be incorrect. The mainstream interpretation of quantum mechanics says that the wave function truly exists, and that a particle exists as a probability of locations defined by the wave function. Only when an observer measures the particle does the particle suddenly "appear" in one physical location. Put another way, when you measure the location of an electron, the measurement process itself randomly picks out one of the possible locations within the wave function for the electron to be located. Scientists call the phenomenon of the particle appearing in one location after it has been measured, "wave function collapse."

While it may seem amazing enough that particles do not exist in a particular location until their wave function collapses, wave functions get even more astounding. A wave function may represent a system that is in more than one position at the same time. To help illustrate this, imagine a quantum system that could be in two possible states—for example, let's say that a particle could be at either location A or location B in space. We don't know whether the particle exists at location A or B until we measure the system. Intuitively, we would say that the particle must really be at either A or B, but we just don't know which one yet. Physicists, though, assume that the particle exists at both A and B at the same time. Only when we measure the system does the particle randomly choose either A or B as its location. Physicists call the ability of a quantum system to be in two or more positions at the same time "superposition."

The reasonable response is to again say that the particle must actually be in only one location, and this whole superposition stuff is nonsense. There are classic experiments, however, that demonstrate that quantum particles are truly in a superposition before they are measured. As you probably learned in science class, light acts as both a wave and as discrete particles called photons. This is called wave-particle duality. The effects of wave-particle duality may be observed in the famous double-slit experiment.

In the double-slit experiment, an observer in a dark room shines a light at a plate that has two small vertical slits cut through it (see Figure 4.1). The observer then places an ordinary sheet of paper several inches behind the plate. Because light acts as a wave, when the waves of light pass through the two slits in the plate, they recombine with each other to produce a series of light

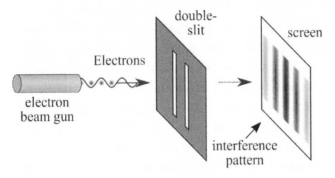

Figure 4.1. In the double-slit experiment, a source fires photons or electrons at a metal plate containing two slits. As the particles pass through the slits they act as waves, forming an interference pattern on the screen behind the plate. NekoJaNekoJa, modified by Johannes Kalliauer, CC BY-SA.

and dark bands on the paper. This shows that the waves of light are interfering with each other to produce an interference pattern on the paper.

Now replace the sheet of paper with a screen that can record the light hitting it. The screen will show that when the light hits it, the light hits at discrete points. In other words, the screen will show that individual photons are hitting the screen. Remember, when we measure a particle, we cause its wave function to collapse and the particle to appear at a single location. The screen measures the photons, causing them to act as though they are choosing a single discrete location when they hit the screen. The interference pattern seen on the sheet of paper will still be observed on the screen, however. This means that the light shined at the plate acts as waves, interfering with each other and causing the interference pattern, but then hits the screen as discrete photon particles. From this the observer can only conclude the existence of wave-particle duality.

We can now tweak the double-slit experiment to also show the existence of superposition. As before, we have a plate with two slits cut in it, and a screen several inches behind it that can record each photon as it hits. Suppose, though, that an observer uses a very weak source of light that allows only one photon at a time to zip toward the plate. A photon fired from the light source will eventually reach the screen behind the plate, where the screen will record the location at which it hit. Now sit back and wait as the observer fires hundreds of thousands of individual photons at the plate.

Amazingly, after a few hundred thousand photons have zoomed toward the plate, one by one, the individual photons hitting the screen begin to form the same interference pattern seen during the first version of the experiment. At first this seems to make absolutely no sense. How can individual photons form an interference pattern?

The answer is that each individual photon travels through both slits in the plate at the same time and interferes with itself. In other words, each photon forms a superposition, and that superposition allows the photon to interfere with itself. When the photon finally hits the screen, the photon randomly chooses one location at which to hit the screen, causing the wave function to collapse, and forming the interference pattern on the screen.

While the result of this experiment may seem like just some weird feature of light, the experiment has also been performed with electrons, atoms, and even molecules consisting of several hundred atoms. The results were the same in each experiment—even molecules of several hundred atoms move through both slits at the same time and interfere with themselves. All particles, not just photons, exhibit wave-particle duality and have the ability to exist in a superposition.

The existence of superpositions inspired the physicist Erwin Schrödinger to come up with the famous thought experiment commonly called Schrödinger's cat. Imagine a cat in a sealed box with an observer outside the box who cannot see or hear the cat. Before placing the cat in the box, the observer has also placed in the box a small amount of a radioactive substance, as well as a Geiger counter, a hammer, and a bottle containing the poisonous gas hydrocyanic acid. The Geiger counter is attached to the hammer, such that if the Geiger counter records that one of the atoms of the radioactive substance has decayed, it will release the hammer. The hammer will then fall and break the bottle, releasing the poison. Needless to say, the fumes from a broken bottle of hydrocyanic acid are fatal to any cats who happen to be placed in a box by a curious observer.

Now let's say the observer leaves the cat in the box for an hour. If during that time the Geiger counter does not record an atom of the radioactive substance decaying, then when the observer opens the box the cat will be alive. If, on the other hand, the Geiger counter does record a radioactive decay, then the hammer will be released, the bottle will break, the poison will fill the box, and when the observer opens the box the cat will be dead.

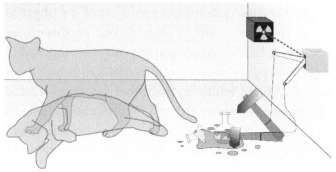

Figure 4.2. In the Schrödinger's cat thought experiment, we don't know whether a radioactive atom has decayed, thereby releasing poison into a box, until we open the box. As a result, while the box remains closed, the cat exists in a superposition—both alive and dead at the same time. Dhatfield, CC BY-SA.

The problem comes from our understanding of the quantum world—until we observe the radioactive substance, the atoms are in a superposition. This means that until we open the box to see whether they have decayed or not, the atoms both have and have not undergone radioactive decay. Furthermore, this means that the Geiger counter both has and has not released the hammer, the poison both has and has not been released into the box, and the cat both is and is not dead inside the box. Put another way, until we open the box and observe the cat, it exists in a superposition, and is both alive and dead at the same time (see Figure 4.2).

The notion that Schrödinger's cat could be both alive and dead at the same time appears fairly ridiculous. In fact, Schrödinger suggested the thought experiment to point out how the quantum explanation of the physical universe does not seem to fit with our experience of reality. There have been several hypotheses proposed to explain how the cat really could be both alive and dead at the same time, while several other hypotheses have been proposed to show that it is merely an illusion to think that the cat could ever exist in a superposition. We must remember, though, that as unintuitive as superpositions may seem, basic experiments you can perform in a college physics lab convincingly show that all particles may exist in superpositions. Schrödinger's cat—both alive and dead—brings the chapter nicely to the first means by which the quantum world may allow life after death.

Many Worlds

Hugh Everett, working on his physics PhD at Princeton University, didn't think it likely that Schrödinger's cat could be both dead and alive at the same time. To overcome the conundrum of superposition, in 1957 Everett proposed the many-worlds interpretation.

The many-worlds interpretation states that all possible outcomes of measuring a wave function exist in their own separate parallel universes. In other words, when we measure a particle that exists in a superposition, one outcome of the measurement becomes one universe, while another outcome of the measurement becomes a different parallel universe. When we open the box to see Schrödinger's cat, the universe splits into two universes—in one universe the cat is dead, in the other universe the cat is alive. Every time an event occurs that causes a wave function to collapse, the universe branches into two or more worlds, with each outcome occurring in its own parallel universe.

According to the many-worlds interpretation, in one parallel universe Schrödinger's cat is alive, and in another parallel universe Schrödinger's cat is dead. Now let's imagine that you are the observer who enjoys doing scientific experiments that put cats in harm's way. When you open the box, the universe splits into two parallel universes. In one universe you find the cat dead, and in the other universe you find that cat alive. This means that every time the universe splits, producing more parallel universes, each parallel universe also contains a parallel version of you. In the many-worlds interpretation there are trillions upon trillions of parallel universes, with new ones being created every second. An uncountable number of those parallel universes contain a version of you. When peering across all the parallel universes, you don't have only one *fetch* running around looking and acting like you but in a different realm of existence, you have trillions of *fetches*.

Unfortunately, in the many-worlds interpretation, the parallel universes do not interact after they have split from each other. Despite the plot twists of roughly a million science fiction stories, a person in one parallel universe cannot jump to a different parallel universe. As amazing as it would be, there is no way for me to travel to the parallel universe where I run a shelter for rescue dogs while also being the king of Norway, kill myself, and then take over my own life. This also means that poor Sir William could not have seen his *fetch* from a parallel universe before he died. It should be noted, though, that even very unlikely events are likely to occur if there are a nearly infinite number of parallel universes. In some parallel universes the life you lead closely resembles your current life, but in other parallel universes your life will have followed a completely different trajectory. In fact, at this very moment in a parallel universe, I am probably having my face licked by a pack of rescued elkhound puppies while on the way to my coronation ceremony.

Objections To The Many-Worlds Interpretation

Consider the number of quantum events occurring in the universe every second, then consider that almost every one of those events leads to the universe branching into two or more parallel universes. Next, consider all the parallel universes that are also undergoing similar branching every single second. That is a lot of parallel universes. Calling the hypothesis the many-worlds interpretation seems to be a bit of an understatement—if the many-worlds interpretation happens to be true, there would be a nearly infinite number of parallel universes constantly bursting into existence (and let's be honest, "infinite-worlds explosion" sounds much cooler than "many-worlds interpretation").

There are dozens of mainstream physicists who believe the many-worlds interpretation best describes the universe—or believe in one of the many variations on the interpretation, often lumped together as multiverse hypotheses. But despite the backing of well-respected physicists, the many-worlds interpretation seems fairly outlandish. Can there really be a nearly infinite number of parallel universes, with trillions of new universes being created every second? Some scientists have called the many-worlds interpretation unscientific because there is no way to test whether it could possibly be true or not. Since parallel universes do not interact after they have branched from each other, there is no way to test for their existence. The core of the scientific method rests on the idea that hypotheses may be falsified through scientific experiments. If there is no way to falsify the many-worlds interpretation, then it is not truly a scientific hypothesis. The cosmologist Paul Davies wrote in 2003 that "invoking an infinity of unseen universes to explain the unusual features of the one we do see is just as ad hoc as invoking an unseen Creator."

While I certainly admit to the validity of the criticisms of the many-worlds interpretation, the arguments of the critics seem to miss the larger point. When considering the very nature of reality and the structure of the universe, ideas that at first seem unscientific may be important in helping us to consider the topology of the possible. We should give serious consideration to the many-worlds interpretation as a potentially insightful way of explaining the very nature of existence.

This places the many-worlds interpretation squarely in the branch of philosophy known as metaphysics. Metaphysics is the philosophical examination of the fundamental nature of reality and being. The many-worlds interpretation may be more metaphysics than science, but nobody should feel ashamed for spending time thinking about the fundamental nature of reality. Besides, any discussion of the afterlife is going to end up leaning at least a little bit on metaphysics!

The Many Worlds Of The Afterlife

Even if the many-worlds interpretation resides more squarely in metaphysics than science, it may still provide a path to the afterlife. Begin by considering that if there truly are a nearly infinite number of parallel universes, then you will not exist in the vast majority of them. In most of the parallel universes you will have never been born. In a large subset of the universes, Earth itself will have never formed.

There will, however, be a significant number of parallel universes in which you do exist. In some of those parallel universes you will already be dead, but in many of them you will still be alive. As a result, there will be a vast number of universes that contain a parallel version of you. As time continues forward, in some of those parallel universes events will occur in which parallel you dies. In many other universes, though, you will remain alive in the branching universes. As the universes continue to branch, there should always be at least one parallel universe in which you remain alive.

This idea may be understood more clearly by again considering Schrödinger's cat. Imagine we leave the cat in the box for several hours with radioactive material that has a high probability of decaying. Very quickly the universe will branch into two parallel universes—one universe where there was radioactive decay and the cat died, and a parallel universe where there was no decay and the cat remained alive. We do not yet open the box, but instead follow the second universe where the cat is still alive. Very soon that universe branches, again producing two more parallel universes, one with a dead cat and one with a living cat. As you can see, the number of parallel universes will increase very quickly, and in most of those universes the cat will be dead, but in at least one parallel universe the cat will remain alive.

Let's return to the start of the cat's time in the box and the first instance that the universe branched. That first branching resulted in two parallel universes, one with a dead cat and one with a living cat. This time, though, let's consider things from the point of view of the cat in the parallel universe where it died. From the view of that cat, it is absolutely dead, its conscious mind having come to a complete and utter halt. However, in the other parallel universe the cat is still very much alive. The dead cat would be forgiven for thinking (if it could still think) that a version of itself had escaped death. In other words, from the point of view of the dead cat, there exists life after death.

The same idea applies to you and me. Over time the number of parallel universes in which you remain alive will get smaller and smaller, but at least you will continue to exist. From the point of view of any parallel universe in which you have died, your continued existence in another parallel universe means that you have achieved the afterlife. The parallel universes in which you are alive will thereby constitute an afterlife for the other versions of you in parallel universes in which you have died.

The originator of the many-worlds interpretation, Hugh Everett, was convinced that his hypothesis meant that he was immortal. As Everett argued, your conscious mind is bound to follow at each branching parallel universe the branch that does not lead to death. Assuming this branching of universes continues forever, at least one version of your conscious mind should be immortal.

But Which You Is Really You?

One version of you may continue to live on for an extremely long time, escaping death at each branching of the parallel universes. There is no guarantee, however, that the version of you in this parallel universe, the version of you reading this sentence, will be the one to win the quantum lottery and continue to exist at each new branching of the universe. In fact, it is much more likely that some other version of you in some other parallel universe will be the one to continue existing far into the future.

This raises the question: If the version of you that continues to live has a completely different history, different memories, different life story, is that person really you? If someone who looks like you and maybe thinks a bit like you achieves immortality, does that mean that the you that you know and love can claim immortality as well? It may be comforting to know that your *fetch* will exist in a parallel universe after you die in this one, but less comforting if the *fetch* shares very few of your memories or personal history.

Even stranger to consider, though, is that there are already trillions of universes in which you have already died. As a consequence, the you in this parallel universe represents the afterlife for those other versions of you that have already died. On occasion we all feel depressed about our lives, or that the world seems to contain nothing but pain and suffering. Perhaps when we start to feel that way, we should try to remember that this life in this universe is the afterlife, and we are lucky to be here.

The next several sections of this chapter explore a very different hypothesis regarding life after death, although it also relies on the workings of the quantum world. In this hypothesis, the afterlife may be achieved through the existence of the quantum mind. To understand the concept of the quantum mind, the chapter must take another brief detour, this time to introduce the idea of quantum entanglement.

Quantum Entanglement

Amazingly, particles in superposition and cats that are both alive and dead at the same time may not be the most bizarre phenomena to emerge from the quantum world. That honor must certainly go to the theory of quantum entanglement. Moreover, while the many-worlds interpretation may or may not explain reality, quantum entanglement is very real and can be studied in any physics lab. In discussing quantum entanglement and the quantum mind, we will return to the assumption that only one universe exists, with no parallel universes.

Quantum entanglement occurs when a pair of particles interact in such a way that the state of one particle becomes dependent on the state of the other particle. This may not seem all that amazing, but it quickly becomes amazing when the particles are separated. Even if they are separated by a vast distance, the state of one of the entangled particles can affect the state of the other faster than the speed of light.

An example makes this much clearer. Suppose a subatomic particle with no spin (i.e., zero spin) decays into two daughter particles, A and B, that are both spinning. Because of the law of conservation of angular momentum, one particle will be spinning up, and to cancel that out and produce a total of zero spin, the other particle will be spinning down. We must remember, though, that until we measure a particle, we merely know the probability of what state the particle will be in. This means that if we measure the spin of particle A, there is a 50 percent chance that it willing be spinning up, and a 50 percent chance that it will be spinning down. Particle A does not actually have an up or down spin until we measure it.

Now suppose we separate particles A and B very far from each other before we measure their directions of spin. Just to be dramatic, we leave particle A on Earth and fly particle B to the moon. At an agreed-upon moment, the scientist on Earth measures the spin of particle A; half a millisecond later, the astronaut on the moon measures the spin of particle B. If the scientist on Earth finds that particle A has an up spin, the astronaut will find that particle B has a down spin. Conversely, if the scientist finds that particle A has a down spin, the astronaut will find that particle B has an up spin. The law of conservation of angular momentum requires this result, and we should not find it at all surprising.

What we should find surprising, though, arises from the very act of measuring the particles. When the scientist on Earth measures particle A, she has a 50 percent chance of finding the particle spinning up, and a 50 percent chance of finding the particle spinning down. The particle, though, does not decide which way it is spinning until the scientist actually measures it. When the scientist measures the spin of particle A, it randomly chooses whether to be spinning up or down. However, once the scientist does measure the spin of particle A, particle B seems to instantaneously know what spin it must have to keep from breaking the law of conservation of angular momentum. Even though the astronaut on the moon measures particle B only half a millisecond after the scientist on Earth measures the spin of particle A, particle B knows whether particle A was spinning up or down, and the astronaut finds particle B spinning in the opposite direction.

This amazing behavior of quantum entanglement does not exist merely as some unproven hypothesis. Physicists have performed many experiments with one observer measuring the state of particle A in one location, and a different observer soon after measuring the state of particle B in a location hundreds of miles away. Because the particles are so far apart, light would not be fast enough to travel between the two particles between when the first observer measured particle A and when the second observer measured particle B. The experiments find, though, that after the measurement of particle A, particle B is always in the correct state—if A spins up, B spins down, and vice versa. It appears that the two entangled particles can somehow communicate with each other faster than the speed of light to make sure that after the measurement of one, the other spins in the correct direction. Albert Einstein famously referred to this astonishing result as "spooky action at a distance."

I imagine most people intuitively want to reject quantum entanglement, and simply assume that at the moment when the two entangled particles were created, they already had a defined state (e.g., A spinning up and

B spinning down). If that were true, then when scientists measure the two particles, they would simply be measuring something already inherent in the particles. Particles that have already decided which way they are spinning when they are created would not be at all remarkable.

Many different experiments, however, have shown that entangled particles don't decide on their spins when they are created. Recall from the discussion of the double-slit experiment earlier in the chapter that before being measured, particles exist solely as wave functions. Particles do not exist in a definite state just waiting for a scientist to measure them. Instead, particles exist as wave functions whose final states are not definite until measured. Only when measured does particle A randomly choose whether to spin up or down, and somehow particle B instantaneously knows this and spins in the opposite direction. All the experiments that have been performed appear to prove that quantum entanglement exists as a real phenomenon, and that there truly is spooky action at a distance.

Entanglement And Biology

While quantum entanglement seems bizarre and something that must occur rarely, or only under ideal conditions in the physics lab, the opposite is true — quantum entanglement occurs whenever particles interact. In fact, for almost every molecule, the many electrons and nuclei making up the molecule are entangled. In the quantum world, unentangled particles are the exception.

If entangled states are so ubiquitous, then we might expect quantum entanglement to play an important role in biology. Unfortunately, biological systems—plants and animals and everything in between—tend to be squishy and difficult to study on a quantum level. Some scientific experiments, though, have come tantalizingly close to showing that biological systems rely on entangled particles to function. For example, in plant cells, the molecules devoted to gathering energy from sunlight during photosynthesis appear to use quantum entanglement. The entanglement of particles in the photosystem complex appears necessary to power the efficient conversion of sunlight into chemical energy.

Not so surprisingly, it turns out that human consciousness is a bit more difficult to understand than photosynthesis. Given the ubiquity of quantum entanglement at the molecular level, though, some scientists have speculated that entanglement may be crucial for producing consciousness—or put differently, that we may each have a quantum mind.

The famous physicist Roger Penrose (or *Sir* Roger Penrose as he is known to you and me), along with anesthesiologist Stuart Hameroff, have proposed a hypothesis of quantum consciousness called Orchestrated Objective Reduction. Fortunately for the longevity of my keyboard, Penrose and Hameroff usually shorten Orchestrated Objective Reduction to Orch OR. I should point out that there are several different hypotheses that posit the necessity of quantum mechanisms for the existence of consciousness. Orch OR remains by far the most famous and well-developed of them, though, and will be the one I discuss in the rest of the chapter.

The Orch OR hypothesis focuses on the protein structures providing the internal scaffolding for neuron cells in the brain. These protein structures are known as microtubules. The Orch OR hypothesis argues that microtubules have electrons that are so close together that the electrons become entangled. The hypothesis then suggests that the entangled states in the scaffolding of one neuron can propagate that entanglement to the scaffolding of other neurons. As a result, the entangled state of one neuron may transmit itself to many other neurons in the brain. Recall that entangled particles seem to be able to share information about their states faster than the speed of light. The Orch OR hypothesis contends that the ability of entangled particles to instantaneously share information allows large regions of our brains to react quickly to incoming stimuli.

Even more important than reacting to stimuli, the Orch OR hypothesis also claims to provide insight on consciousness. Under Orch OR, when one particle in the microtubule scaffolding undergoes wave collapse, the other particles entangled with that particle also collapse. Penrose and Hameroff argue that the collapsing of these wave particles are themselves what create moments of consciousness. Put another way, in the Orch OR hypothesis, only through the quantum entanglement of particles in our neurons do we achieve conscious thought.

This should immediately raise the question of why we have neurons shooting neurotransmitters at each other all the time if consciousness doesn't depend on the connections of these neurons but instead relies on the quantum entanglement of electrons in microtubules. Under the Orch OR hypothesis, the connections of the neurons and their release of neurotransmitters provide for the housekeeping requirements of the brain—reminding us to breathe, coordinating muscular movements, maintaining bodily homeostasis. The stuff our brains need to do to keep us alive depends on the connections of our neurons and the release of neurotransmitters. Consciousness, though, arises from the entangled states of the microtubules within those neurons.

Orch OR And The Afterlife

The idea that consciousness arises from the entangled state of particles in microtubules would be interesting enough; the Orch OR hypothesis, though, might also have something to say about the afterlife. In an interview, Hameroff stated, "Let's say the heart stops beating, the blood stops flowing, the microtubules lose their quantum state. The quantum information within the microtubules is not destroyed, it can't be destroyed, it just distributes and dissipates to the universe at large." Hameroff then added, "If the patient is resuscitated, revived, this quantum information can go back into the microtubules and the patient says 'I had a near death experience.'" Hameroff finished the interview by saying, "If they're not revived, and the patient dies, it's possible that this quantum information can exist outside the body, perhaps indefinitely, as a soul."

In a book chapter written with Deepak Chopra, Hameroff argues that the entangled particles in the microtubules warp space-time geometry, and that this warping, along with the collapse of wave functions in the brain, allows us to experience consciousness.[4] When the brain dies, the warped space-time geometry remains, and the consciousness of the brain continues to exist in a different plane of space-time geometry. Hameroff contends that when people die, their consciousness exists for eternity in the very geometry of the universe. The quantum mind creates a quantum soul.

If the process by which quantum consciousness creates a quantum soul seems a bit fuzzy to you, you are not alone. The primary criticism leveled against quantum consciousness and quantum immortality is the same as the one leveled against the many-worlds interpretation—that it appears to be untestable and is therefore not truly a scientific hypothesis. Some scientists refer to claims of quantum entanglement giving rise to consciousness as nothing more than quantum mysticism. By simply invoking quantum mechanics, any quack or New Age healer can make claims about the workings of the universe, even if there exists no evidence for those claims. The physicist Victor Stenger has said that quantum consciousness has no scientific basis and "should take its place along with gods, unicorns and dragons."

I feel it important to note that while Penrose has written scientific papers with Hameroff about Orch OR, he has not signed off on the idea that Orch OR allows for quantum immortality. As mentioned above, Hameroff's proposal that Orch OR may lead to a quantum afterlife was made in a book chapter with Deepak Chopra. Chopra is an alternative-medicine advocate well known in the New Age movement. Chopra has claimed that "quantum healing" can cure disease, and that aging may be controlled by one's state of mind. Chopra certainly advocates quantum mysticism. The fact that Hameroff published his ideas on quantum immortality with Chopra calls into question the seriousness of his hypothesis for a quantum afterlife.

Unfortunately, at this point in our understanding of quantum mechanics, the quantum soul and quantum immortality of the Orch OR hypothesis appear to fall squarely within the orbit of quantum mysticism.

Living The Quantum Life

While no scientific research currently supports the Orch OR hypothesis, other research clearly points to the possibility that quantum effects play at least a small role in biological processes. Future research may very well support the importance of quantum mechanics in allowing us to experience consciousness. Of course, the leap from quantum mechanics being necessary for consciousness to the existence of a quantum afterlife remains pretty large. On the other hand, 150 years ago, the idea that particles could be in two places at once would have been laughed at as utter rubbish, and probably derided as nonscientific mysticism. I certainly would not want to place any bets on what "mysticisms" from today will be considered scientifically valid in 150 years.

The many-worlds interpretation, though, remains on much stronger scientific ground. Many well-respected physicists believe that the many-worlds interpretation is possible, if not downright likely. Quantum mechanics are weird, and a weird hypothesis may be just what is needed to explain it all. If so, then when you die in this universe, there should still be multitudes of other universes in which you remain alive. The many-worlds interpretation suggests that when we die, we will survive in not just one afterlife, but in trillions of them.

CHAPTER 5

UPLOADING THE DEAD

E very family has at least one person who loves studying genealogy. Among my relatives, the honor of biggest genealogy buff goes to my cousin Sharon. At every family reunion Sharon pulls out a giant piece of paper, covering the entire picnic table, displaying our complete family tree. She likes to point in triumph to the names of the new ancestors she's been able to add since the last reunion. I sometimes wonder how the latest ancestors inserted into the tree would feel knowing that what exists of the memory of their lives is little more than a name added to a sheet of paper, nearly hidden by a bowl of potato salad.

Sharon loves adding ancestors to the family tree, but can you imagine how excited she would be if she could actually speak to those ancestors? Imagine how excited you would be if you could hear the stories of the outlaws and lawmen, the heretics and propagandists, who contributed to the branching of your family tree. If it were possible, I bet almost everyone would choose to resurrect the minds of their ancestors—to hear their stories, or simply to spend time with loved ones who had already died. While it isn't yet a reality, it may be possible in the near future to bring back to life the minds of those who have died.

Understanding how we may one day be able to peer into the past to resurrect the minds of the dead requires another brief trip into the quantum realm.

Quantum Computing

In the classical computers that most of us are familiar with, the computer stores information in its memory. The computer stores this memory as strings of billions or trillions of "bits." Each bit is either a 0 or a 1, and the arrangement of the bits determines the memory of the computer. We define the number of bits needed to completely describe the memory of the computer as the size of the memory.

Quantum computers, however, are very different. Recall from Chapter 4 that a particle does not have to be in only one state or another—a particle may be in a superposition where it exists in several different states at the same time. In a standard computer like the ones we know, each bit exists as only a 0 or a 1. In a quantum computer, though, the bits are particles that are in superpositions—the bits can be more than just 0 or 1. Computer scientists call these quantum bits qubits. As you may have guessed, going from a standard computer to a quantum computer vastly increases computing power.

With the amazing computing power possible with a quantum computer, what should we do first with it? Mucking about with time seems like a good place to start. Fortunately, given physicists' current understanding of the universe, it does not appear that time travel will ever be possible (for the sake of this chapter, I will assume that the block universe hypothesis of Chapter 3, which suggests that all time exists simultaneously, does not apply). There are the occasional hypotheses that pop up claiming to have found a way time travel could occur, but often those hypotheses are shown to have mistaken assumptions or to be extremely unlikely. The arrow of time seems to go in only one direction.

While we may never be able to force the arrow of time to fly backward, it may be possible to at least figure out where it has been. In an experiment in 2019, scientists used a quantum computer to simulate a particle moving backward in time. This might not seem all that impressive at first, but you have to remember that before we measure a particle, it exists as a wave function that represents all the possible states of the particle. As time moves forward, the wave function for the particle spreads out. To simulate the wave function going backward in time, coalescing instead of spreading, is no easy task. Imagine you have thrown a rock into a pond, and you are watching the ripples spread out across the water. If you wanted to rewind what you had just seen, to convincingly simulate those ripples moving backward across the pond toward the rock, you would need a pretty powerful computer. Now imagine doing that for the wave function of a subatomic particle spreading out through space.

The most amazing aspect of the 2019 experiment was that the scientists were able to accomplish it using a quantum computer composed of only two qubits. Quantum computing currently dwells in its infancy — the most advanced quantum computers scientists have built consist of only a handful of qubits. Once all the kinks have been worked out, though, quantum computers should be able to perform tasks in a matter of minutes that would take a classical supercomputer thousands of years to finish.

When scientists in the future gain the ability to harness the computing power of quantum computers, the desire to simulate more than just a single particle moving backward in time seems likely. While it may seem incredible to contemplate now, in the future, humans may be able to follow the arrow of time backward, simulating in fine detail the distant past. The follow-up question then becomes, what will humans in the future do with the ability to peer into the past?

Uploading The Dead

In Chapter 2, I argued that scientists in the future will likely be able to simulate human consciousness in a computer. Admittedly, such simulations may be complex enough that they require the processing power of a quantum computer, but there seems to be no reason why the connections in the brain could not be simulated in a computer to create virtual consciousness. I then followed this argument to its logical conclusion, suggesting that that ability to simulate consciousness in the future suggests that we are living in a computer right now.

Assume for the sake of this chapter, however, that we are real humans and not simulated beings. When scientists do perfect virtual consciousness in the future, many people hope there will be an incredible side-benefit to the humans alive at that time. The ability to simulate consciousness in a computer may allow a person in the future to upload his or her mind into a computer right after death. Uploading a mind would allow that consciousness to exist for thousands or millions of years in a virtual afterlife. Futurists call this idea mind uploading.

The idea behind mind uploading is quite simple: immediately after a person dies, the location and connections of each neuron in that person's brain are precisely mapped. Scientists then recreate a map of the deceased person's brain in a computer. The computer uses that map of the brain to create a virtual consciousness that should be nearly identical to the consciousness of the person when she was alive. Every important characteristic of the dead person's mind— thoughts, feelings, memories—should continue to exist in the computer. The person who has died finds life after death within the computer simulation.

Mind uploading may one day be possible, but that one day seems pretty far in the future. The fact that mind uploading may only be available far in the future seems really unfair, though. Does everyone who dies after mind uploading becomes routine get to enjoy a virtual afterlife, while everyone who dies before then — including everyone alive right now — does not?

As you've probably already figured out, the reason I discussed the ability of quantum computers to look back in time was so that I could answer the preceding question with a big NO! If quantum computers become powerful enough to follow the arrow of time backward, then it may be possible to map the neural connections — the consciousness — of every mind that has ever existed.

The process would be similar to mind uploading, but just include an extra step. Scientists would use a quantum computer to peer into the past, allowing them to decipher the neural connections of every human brain existing through time as they look farther and farther back. The maps for each of these minds would then be placed into a computer simulation, creating a virtual consciousness for every human. It should not matter if a person died days ago or millennia ago; by looking far enough into the past, scientists would be able to reconstruct every individual human consciousness and upload it into the computer simulation. This means that even if you live before scientists are capable of uploading minds, after you die you will wake up hundreds of years in the future, your mind recreated and simulated in a computer. You will have gained a digital afterlife.

The idea of uploading the minds of those who have long since died has been proposed independently by several people, including physicists Frank Tipler and David Deutsch, and computer scientists Giulio Prisco and Hans Moravec. They each came to the conclusion that future civilizations will be capable of peering into the past, and will desire to recreate the conscious mind of every person who has ever lived.

Who Gets Uploaded?

Reconstructing the past to upload the conscious minds of the dead would be a huge undertaking, requiring enormous time and resources. Would a future civilization be interested in devoting so much wealth to reviving dead minds? Obviously, we have little idea what principles and morals a future civilization might prioritize. However, I believe the general discussion in Chapter 2 on a future human civilization respecting human consciousness, no matter its form, applies here as well. Throughout all of history, humanity has held great respect for the lives and minds of human beings. A future civilization will almost certainly continue to respect and be fascinated by the lives of those who came before them. A future civilization would at the very least express a strong desire to resurrect the minds of the most famous people who have ever lived. We can be certain that even far in the future, people will want to speak with Abraham Lincoln or Mahatma Gandhi. Once the minds of the famous and infamous have been brought back to simulated life, it seems likely there would be a strong desire to continue mapping the minds of the dead, until every person who has ever lived could be given a digital afterlife.

Imagine my cousin Sharon, living hundreds of years in the future. After the minds of Golda Meir and Brad Pitt have been resurrected, and my cousin has had a chance to listen to their stories, she would almost certainly have an unquenchable longing to hear the stories of her direct ancestors. Writing down an ancestor's name on an overgrown family tree is nothing compared to resurrecting that ancestor.

What Would The Virtual Afterlife Be Like?

In Chapter 2, I discussed the possibility that we are all digital creatures, living as science experiments in a simulated universe. I argued that if our conscious minds were created for use in a computer model, the scientists who programmed us would likely feel an obligation to reward the minds they created. That sense of obligation, though, would likely be lessened by the fact that our simulated brains were created for a computer model and never existed in the physical universe. The scientists who programmed us may be willing to reward us with an afterlife, but winning the next round of grant funding would definitely be a higher priority.

The situation, though, would be entirely different if the simulated minds in the afterlife were the direct ancestors of the scientists creating that afterlife. Ask yourself, if you were designing an afterlife for your direct ancestors, as well as the most brilliant and interesting people who ever existed (not that the two groups are mutually exclusive, although they definitely don't overlap in my family), wouldn't you try to make the afterlife you design as comfortable and interesting as possible? Wouldn't you try to create a true paradise? Perhaps more importantly, if you know that when you die you will also be uploaded into the afterlife you have designed, wouldn't you attempt to make it the greatest, most wonderful experience imaginable? The scientists and artists tasked with inventing the simulated afterlife for every human who has ever existed, as well as themselves when they die, would probably do their best to design a paradise that would rival the most spectacular heaven any god might conceive of.

It may also be safe to presume that if a future human civilization goes to the trouble of resurrecting dead minds and uploading them into a virtual afterlife, that civilization will want to make sure the afterlife exists for as long as possible. As mentioned in Chapter 2, a computer can calculate much faster than a human mind can think, so hundreds or thousands of years may pass in a simulated paradise for every year that passes in the physical world. A simulated mind in the afterlife may be there for what feels like millions or even billions of years. Hopefully the designers of the digital paradise are talented enough that even a billion years of conscious thought does not seem long enough.

But Is It Really You?

As I already asked in the last chapter, when are you no longer you? If your physical, biological body dies, but scientists create a computer simulation of the connections that make up your mind, is that simulation really you? To start examining this question, I begin by asking a slightly different one: What would the bodies in paradise look like?

I think it safe to assume that if a future civilization goes to the trouble of creating a paradise for every person who has ever lived, they wouldn't force the reconstructed minds to simply float around as brains without bodies. Surely a simulated paradise would include a body for every person placed in the afterlife. When peering back through time to map the brains of dead humans, the scientists doing the mapping would certainly be able to reconstruct the outer appearance of the body carrying that brain. But given that these newly mapped minds are going to paradise, would the bodies of the future simply be exact recreations of the bodies we had when we died?

More likely, each person would be given a version of their body when they were young and in peak physical condition. Of course, there are some of us who weren't in peak physical condition, even when we were young. What kind of body would we receive? Perhaps every mind recreated in paradise would be gifted with a perfect body to carry it around—a physically beautiful body that never feels pain or sickness. But who gets to decide what the perfect body looks like? More importantly, if you are given a perfect body that differs significantly from the body you had when you were alive, and that never knows pain, it would almost certainly change the workings of your brain.

Consider how frequently your body influences your conscious thoughts—perhaps you sense your back beginning to feel tired, so you change how you are sitting; or you notice that the fingers on your right hand feel slightly cold, so you rub them to warm them up. More crucially, fear of pain or sickness frequently changes how we consciously move our bodies and interact with the environment—there is no need to stand away from the edge of the cliff if you have a body that cannot feel pain. To change the relationship between the body and the mind would almost certainly change the consciousness attached to that body. Are you truly the same person you were before if your mind exists in a different body?

Moving beyond the connection between body and mind, we must also ask whether a brain that has been meticulously mapped and simulated in a computer produces a consciousness identical to the original biological brain. This question gets at what we humans actually believe ourselves to be. When I reflect on myself as an individual, I consider the true essence of who I am to reside in my thoughts, feelings, and memories. I certainly find it interesting from a scientific perspective to understand what physical processes allow me to be conscious, but as long as I am conscious, I don't really care overly much how it happens. If a future civilization peers into the past and simulates the conscious thoughts and memories of a person who has died, then I imagine most of us would consider that to be a resurrection of the actual person.

This conclusion should be bolstered by the likely experience of someone who has died in the past, and then been simulated in the future. An individual who has died and then been digitally recreated won't realize the delay in his rebirth. The person may have died a thousand years in the past, and be resurrected a thousand years from now, but to him, there would be no time spent dead. The person would die, and then wake up immediately in the digital paradise—it would be as though no time had passed between death and rebirth. The person being simulated would almost certainly feel as if the digital recreation is a true continuation of his mind.

Some will argue, however, that a simulated brain can never genuinely replicate the living thing. So far in this chapter, I have assumed that a computer can recreate the human mind, but perhaps the nature of consciousness requires that it arise only in a biological system. Most neuroscientists would disagree, arguing that eventually a computer will be able to simulate consciousness. Their logic is straightforward—the human mind and the consciousness it produces are explained by physical laws, and computers do a good job of simulating physical laws. Scientists will eventually understand the neurons in the brain just as well as any other cell in the body. By understanding the connections between neurons, we will someday understand everything there is to know about consciousness. Once that day arrives, simulating a conscious mind within a computer will almost certainly be possible.

Despite the pronouncements of neuroscientists, there are many scientists and philosophers who believe that it will never be possible to simulate consciousness within a computer. Most of those who make this argument claim that consciousness appears to be unique within the universe and does not currently fit within the known laws of physics. What removes consciousness from the laws of physics depends on the person making the argument. One popular version argues that the uniqueness of consciousness stems from the ability of the conscious mind to change the physical world by deciding what to observe and what not to observe. While initially this seems extremely profound, there exists no evidence that human consciousness changes the physical world in ways that nonconscious phenomena cannot. At this point in our scientific understanding, it certainly appears that computers will eventually be able to simulate human consciousness.

But this unfortunately raises an even more vexing question: How do we know whether a mind, uploaded into a computer and appearing to be fully conscious, truly is conscious? A mind being simulated in a computer may display all the outward signs of being conscious, but the computer program may just be really good at mimicking the signs of consciousness without actually creating a conscious mind. We may propose one obvious solution—simply ask the mind that has been uploaded into the computer if she is conscious. If she answers with a clear "yes," we may be satisfied that the computer has simulated a conscious mind. But it could just as easily be the case that she answered "yes" because the computer program made her answer yes, and there was no conscious decision behind that response.

This problem stretches far beyond computers simulating human minds, however. Consciousness is a fundamentally subjective experience—while I know that I am conscious, there is no way for me to prove to someone else that I am conscious, or for someone else to prove to me that he is conscious. In my daily life, I must accept that the people I interact with who appear to be conscious truly are conscious. Similarly, for a mind uploaded into a computer, if such a mind appears to be conscious, then perhaps we will simply have to accept that it genuinely is conscious. Put another way, those who argue that a computer will never simulate consciousness may be correct, but if we are willing to accept that human brains other than our own create consciousness then we have no reason to hold a computer to a higher standard.

Stuck In A Robot

So far in this chapter I have assumed that scientists would place recreated minds in a computer simulation. This might not be at all what a future civilization decides to do with its dead ancestors. Instead of uploading minds to a computer simulation, perhaps future scientists will place those minds into physical bodies.

There are two types of physical bodies that a scientist would be most likely to use: a biological body, or a humanoid robot. Placing an uploaded mind into a biological body seems unlikely. Doing so would require growing neurons to exactly replicate the neurons and their connections that existed in the brain of the dead person. Perhaps in the future such a task will be possible, but the time and effort needed to grow brains for the billions of humans who have died throughout history makes the undertaking seem unlikely.

Much more likely is the possibility of uploading minds into humanoid robots. Admittedly, the mind being uploaded would still end up in a computer, but in this case a computer stuck inside a robot. A humanoid robot would be able to move about the physical world, interacting with the environment in the same way that a living human could. Such an uploaded mind would not get to experience a simulated paradise, but would instead get to exist in the world as if truly resurrected from the dead.

The greatest flaw in such a plan, of course, comes from the fact that uploading every single human who has ever existed into his or her own robot would require vastly more resources than uploading those minds into a computer simulation. A computer could potentially hold billions of minds, while each robot could only hold one mind. Additionally, there would likely be little room on Earth for billions of new robots to roam around—just imagine the lines at the robot version of Starbucks.

Simply as a way to conserve resources and physical space, it seems much more likely that scientists would place any recreated minds within a simulated paradise instead of within a physical body. For those whose minds are uploaded, though, the difference between a computer simulation and a physical body may be negligible. As long as we believe ourselves to be conscious, and we have bodies to move around in, a simulated paradise may actually be preferable to the real world (with all its pesky laws of physics that can't be undone with a few lines of computer code).

Do You Upload Hitler?

Assume for a moment that the mind of every person who has ever lived could be uploaded into a simulated afterlife. An important ethical question arises: *Should* the mind of every person who has ever lived be uploaded?

As the heading of this section suggests, do monsters such as Adolf Hitler or Pol Pot deserve to be resurrected in a digital paradise? I imagine most people would answer that no, such people do not deserve to have their conscious minds reborn. But then the question becomes, who gets to decide who enjoys the afterlife and who does not? Does every person convicted of murder get rejected from paradise? What about everyone who cheated on their taxes, are they left out as well?

Figure 5. Bearbaiting as practiced in the time of Queen Elizabeth I. From *Cassell's Illustrated History of England, Volume 2*, by John Cassell. Public domain.

Let's say there are judges who decide who gains admission to paradise and who does not. Do these judges make their decisions based on an understanding of the ethics and morals of the time the judges are alive, or those of the time the resurrected person lived? For example, most people born in the twenty-first century consider bearbaiting completely reprehensible. Bearbaiting consisted of placing a bear in a pit, where it was chained by the neck or leg to a post. The sport part came from releasing several bulldogs to attack the chained bear (see Figure 5). The bulldogs had been trained to try to kill the bear, while the bear, defending itself, would try to kill the bulldogs (with one or the other often succeeding). Unfortunately, bearbaiting was a very popular sport throughout much of human history. In fact, Queen Elizabeth I was such a fan of the sport that she overruled Parliament's attempt to ban bearbaiting on Sundays. If judging by the morality of our time, would we forbid anyone who enjoyed a bearbaiting contest, even Queen Elizabeth I, from entering paradise? Would we instead judge individuals based on the morality of the time period in which they lived, and let anyone living in the sixteenth century who enjoyed bearbaiting into paradise?

The safest course would be to simply upload the consciousness of every person who has ever lived, whether saint or villain. For the villains that escaped punishment during their lifetimes, though, maybe they would be sentenced to a period of punishment before being allowed to enter paradise. Indeed, there could be different levels of punishment based on the evilness of the deeds a person committed while alive. Nine levels of punishment somehow seems appropriate. Perhaps in the ninth level, the truly vile such as Hitler and Pol Pot could be frozen in blocks of ice with only their heads sticking out in order that their screams might escape. Somehow, I think Dante would approve.

Not surprisingly, uploading minds and then deciding whether to punish them or not raises many of the same questions as deciding whether those minds should simply be denied entry into paradise in the first place. Who gets to determine the appropriate punishment for people who lived hundreds or thousands of years in the past? If a civilization in the future is willing to undertake the effort and expense of recreating all human minds, does that automatically mean they have the right to punish some of those minds however they see fit? Are you willing to hope for an afterlife if that means letting some random person from the future judge your entire life? Suddenly, an all-knowing god who makes those kinds of decisions almost seems like a welcome relief!

Where To Put Your Faith

There seems little reason to doubt that scientists in the future will one day be able to simulate human consciousness. If so, simulating biological brains within a computer also seems eminently possible. In other words, mind uploading appears to be only a matter of time.

The greater difficulty lies in peering back into the past with enough clarity to reconstruct brains that lived centuries or millennia ago. Reversing the arrow of time will always remain the greatest challenge humans face. I have no doubt future human civilizations will achieve amazing scientific breakthroughs, but seeing backward in time may be too much for even those sophisticated civilizations.

Hoping to awake after death in a digital paradise means placing your faith in the genius of a future human society. Sadly, placing your faith in future humans may not be any more reasonable than placing your faith in a god. On the other hand, there is plenty of evidence that humans exist, and no evidence that a god exists, so maybe placing your faith in the genius of humanity is a bit less dubious.

This does raise an interesting possibility, though, briefly mentioned in the Introduction. In the Christian religious tradition, individuals have souls that depart the body on death and then ascend to heaven. Most Christians think of heaven as a paradise free of all hardship. If a future human civilization does create a simulated paradise, and uploads into that paradise the mind of every human who has ever lived, does that fulfill the promise of God in the Bible to bring the souls of the dead to heaven? Would the religious faithful accept a human-created paradise as what God meant when He promised heaven? The Bible often states that God works through humans—perhaps most Christians would be willing to accept a simulated paradise as the reward God promised. On the other hand, any simulated paradise would most likely be marred by a simulated religious war or two (or three or a thousand). Although, to be fair, after being in a digital paradise for a few million years, the occasional religious war might provide some valuable entertainment.

CHAPTER 6

OPEN INDIVIDUALISM

Theseus was the founder and first king of Athens, and also someone who never existed. Alright, it's possible he existed, but it's extremely unlikely that he killed a Minotaur (half man, half bull) living in the center of a labyrinth in Crete. Equally unlikely are the stories of Theseus killing King Cercyon in a wrestling match, sacrificing the giant Marathonian Bull to the gods, and murdering at least one enraged centaur (half man, half horse). Figure 6 shows an ancient Greek cup depicting just a few of Theseus's supposed adventures. Despite allegedly killing several fantastical monsters, Theseus's greatest contribution to humanity comes not from his ability to slay imaginary animals, but from a philosophical paradox named for his ship.

The Roman historian Plutarch wrote about Theseus's ship in the book, *Life of Theseus*. Plutarch wrote that after killing the Minotaur on the island of Crete, Theseus sailed his ship back to Athens. The Athenian people

Figure 6. The deeds of Theseus painted on a *kylix* (ancient Greek cup for drinking wine), from approximately 440–430 BCE. In the center of the *kylix*, Theseus can be seen slaying the Minotaur. Given he performed so many amazing deeds, leaving Theseus's ship in a harbor for several centuries makes perfect sense. British Museum, CC BY-SA.

were so enraptured by the heroic deeds of Theseus that they kept his ship in the Athenian harbor as a memorial to the great man. According to Plutarch, the people of Athens left the ship sitting in the harbor undisturbed for several centuries.

Ships built during the time Theseus lived — or at least the time he was supposed to have lived — were of course made of wood. Wood sitting in the salt water of a harbor for several centuries will eventually begin to decay. Plutarch wrote in his history that the Athenians solved the problem of the rotting wood quite elegantly; the ship "was preserved by the Athenians down even to the time of Demetrius Phalereus, for they took away the old planks as they decayed, putting in new and stronger timber in their places."

Ancient philosophers quickly understood the paradox in this story. Each piece of wood in Theseus's ship would eventually decay and be replaced by a new piece of wood. When every plank of wood used to build Theseus's ship had been replaced, would the ship that remained still be the ship of Theseus? If no piece of wood in the ship had made the voyage to Crete and back, if Theseus had not walked across a single plank, how could anyone still call it Theseus's ship?

Unsurprisingly, this philosophical paradox just raised more questions. How many planks of wood had to be replaced before we could no longer claim the ship in the harbor was the original ship? Most of us would probably agree that after replacing only one plank, the ship of Theseus was still the original ship. But what about when 25 percent of the planks had been replaced? What about 51 percent?

Several centuries later, the philosopher Thomas Hobbes added a new wrinkle to the ship of Theseus paradox. Suppose that as the ancient Greeks removed each original plank of wood from the ship and replaced it with stronger wood, they stored the original planks in a warehouse. Then suppose that modern technology became advanced enough that the decay infecting those planks could be fixed, such that each plank of wood was returned to its former strength. Craftsmen could then easily reassemble those restored planks in the warehouse to rebuild a ship. The question then becomes, which ship is the true ship of Theseus—the one in the harbor that has always been called the ship of Theseus, even though it contains none of the original planks of wood, or the new ship in the warehouse, built out of the original planks? Would the answer change if the original planks were treated to rid them of decay in such a way that each plank consisted of the original wood fibers plus glue or plastic holding those fibers in place? In other words, are the original planks still original if they are only partially original, and what does that mean for the ship built from them?

Amazingly, the ship of Theseus paradox plays an important role in helping us understand the paradox of human consciousness and identity. Consider that as you move from second to second, the structure of your brain constantly changes—neurons are getting ready to release neurotransmitters or have just released neurotransmitters, synapses are changing as new memories form, new neurons are being created and integrated into the structure of your brain. These continuous changes mean that as each new moment in time arrives, your brain is not the same brain it was a moment ago.

If we assume that your brain determines your consciousness, then your consciousness also changes from each moment to the next. As most of us will agree, we think of our consciousness as the essence of who we are, our true self. The ship of Theseus paradox suggests, though, that if your brain is not the same brain it was a moment ago, and your consciousness is not the same consciousness it was a moment ago, then you are not the same you that you were a moment ago. The planks of your mind change every second, meaning that every second creates a new version of you.

This of course seems completely outside of our intuition and experience. I believe I am the same person I was a moment ago, and I even believe that I am fundamentally the same person I was as a child. But if my consciousness changes every second, and the underlying brain structures that determine that consciousness change every second, then what exactly remains the same? Why do I find it so intuitively easy to believe that I am the same person from second to second and year to year?

As this discussion of consciousness suggests, at this roughly midway point in the book, I will be turning from science to philosophy. Unlike the previous chapters, the ideas in this chapter are not grounded in scientific hypotheses and experimental predictions. Nevertheless, the concepts discussed in this chapter are worthy of serious consideration. Philosophers have been contemplating questions about life after death for millennia, and philosophy has interesting things to say about the possibility of the afterlife for those of us who don't believe in God. A philosophical idea called open individualism attempts to confront head-on the ship of Theseus paradox as it relates to consciousness. A byproduct of this attempt just happens to be a philosophical premise for the possibility of life after death.

Closed, Empty, Or Open

Philosophers have proposed numerous ways to explain how a constantly changing mind maintains the same personal identity. Any possible explanation must satisfy both our intuitive sense of ourselves and the ship of Theseus paradox inherent in our continuously changing brains. As the last section suggested, the idea of open individualism seems to do a good job of reconciling these issues.

The term open individualism gained its name from the philosopher Daniel Kolak. In his 2004 book, *I Am You: The Metaphysical Foundations for Global Ethics*, Kolak suggested three ways of explaining personal identity: closed individualism, empty individualism, and open individualism. Each version of individualism suggests a different understanding of consciousness. To best grasp the idea of open individualism, it helps to first understand closed and empty individualism. The following sections describe these three possible versions of conscious identity.

Closed Individualism

Closed individualism best resembles our intuitive, common-sense understanding of our own personal identity. Under the closed individualism view, you begin to exist when you are born, and you cease to exist when your consciousness no longer exists. For the period in between, closed individualism states that while you may change through time, your basic identity continues to exist from moment to moment. In other words, there is only one you, and you exist as a single individual moving through time.

Clearly, the main problem with closed individualism comes from the fact that it does nothing to grapple with the ship of Theseus paradox. If we acknowledge that a person's brain, and therefore consciousness, changes from moment to moment, then what exactly is the identity that exists from each moment to the next? Like the ship of Theseus with nearly all its planks replaced, the structure and function of your brain today differs almost entirely from the structure and function of your brain when you were a baby. How can you seriously claim that you have the same identity today as when you were a newborn?

While closed individualism holds that when your consciousness ends your personal identity also ends, that does not mean that closed individualism implies there can be no life after death. Closed individualism only states that you cease to exist when your consciousness ceases. This means that if any version of your consciousness exists—perhaps within a computer simulation or a block universe—then you continue to exist.

Empty Individualism

Empty individualism does a better job of directly confronting the ship of Theseus paradox. Under empty individualism, you only exist for a single moment in time, and in every new moment in time, a new you exists. Put another way, in each and every moment in time, a new you is born, lives, and dies. This birth, life, and death continually repeats itself every second in which you (or at least some version of you that closely resembles you) exists.

The empty individualism view of the ship of Theseus paradox would hold that every time the ancient Greeks replaced a plank of wood in the ship, a new ship was born. As a result, there was no single ship of Theseus, or even two or three; every change to the ship resulted in the death of an old ship and the birth of a new ship. Similarly, every change in the structure of your brain, every new thought, creates a new you. You live and die in every moment.

The empty individualism view closely resembles the block universe hypothesis from Chapter 3. According to the block universe hypothesis, every moment in time exists simultaneously, just as every location in space exists simultaneously. In the block universe, a person consciously inhabits every moment of his life simultaneously. Empty individualism and the block universe hypothesis therefore make the same prediction—at every moment in time, a conscious version of you exists that experiences only that single moment.

Empty individualism and the block universe hypothesis do not overlap completely, though. In the block universe hypothesis, each moment of your life exists simultaneously for eternity, meaning that you experience each moment for eternity. However, that does not necessarily mean that each moment in which you exist contains a different version of you. When you move from your kitchen to your living room, you are moving to a different point in space, but that does not mean that your personal identity has necessarily changed when you move from one location to another. Similarly, simply because every moment of time coexists in a block does not necessarily mean that your personal identity at those different moments in time has changed simply because you are in a different temporal location. Under empty individualism, however, each new moment creates a new person with a new identity.

The primary problem with empty individualism arises from how it seems to completely disagree with our intuitive sense of ourselves. Even though I may logically realize that the person I am today is very different from the person I was as a teenager or as a baby, I still feel strongly that those previous versions of me are all still me. I instinctively believe in the continuation of my personal identity through time.

This instinctive belief leaves us with a problem: closed individualism explains the intuitive sense that we are the same conscious being moving through time, but cannot explain what that being consists of in a way that satisfies the ship of Theseus paradox; conversely, empty individualism explains the ship of Theseus paradox, but cannot explain the common-sense feeling that I am one unique person moving through time. As you may have already guessed, the open individualism view of personal identity comes to the rescue.

Open Individualism

Under open individualism, what we think of as our personal identity turns out to be an illusion. The consciousness that I call me, and the consciousness that you call you, are not really two separate identities. Instead, there exists only one force that creates the personal identities of every human.

This idea immediately strikes most people as pretty strange, so perhaps I should start with an analogy. Imagine you are in a library, aimlessly wandering among the shelves of books. You randomly stop and pick up a novel, opening the book to a page somewhere in the middle of the story. You happen upon a page describing a young girl about to ride a horse for the first time. Assuming the writing is decent, in your mind you will be transported to the viewpoint of the little girl, feeling her fear and excitement as she gathers her courage to clamber onto the back of the horse. Putting that book down, you move on, randomly stopping again to pick up another book. This time you become a middle-aged detective about to get punched in the nose for asking the wrong questions. With each book you pick up, you briefly become a character in the novel, seeing the world through his or her eyes. With just a few words on a page, your mind animates the personal identities of the characters in the books. As simple as opening a book, you breathe life into a personal identity; as simple as closing a book, the personal identity goes dormant, waiting patiently for a new mind to bring it back into existence.

Similar to books in a library, open individualism holds that our conscious minds are animated by a being or entity outside of us. Just like the characters in the books, we are not conscious beings by ourselves — we require something outside of us to gives us the illusion of a personal identity. As a consequence, our personal identity does not reside within our physical body, but instead resides within the being animating us.

To extend the analogy of the library, consider an ethereal being walking around London. The people on the busy streets are perfectly normal, made of flesh and blood, and with brains that control their actions. Each of those brains, though, may be thought of as a novel. Like words on a page, the neurons are connected in specific ways to produce thoughts and hold memories, but like a book, each brain is merely a collection of molecules that has no consciousness of its own. The being walking through the city randomly stops next to a person. Like picking up a book, the being enters the mind of the person, animating that person's consciousness for a few minutes. The being then moves on to the next person, entering that brain and becoming that consciousness for a bit. To this ethereal being, the whole of Earth is a library, and each mind a novel.

Open individualism does not require that the being or entity become only one identity at a time, though. Instead, the being can animate all conscious minds at the same time. As a result, under open individualism, we each have our own conscious experience, but the animating force for our individual consciousness also animates every other consciousness.

The philosophical importance of open individualism lies in its ability to overcome the weaknesses inherent in empty and closed individualism. First, open individualism explains our intuitive belief that we are the same person with the same identity from moment to moment, or even from year to year. Unlike empty individualism, which holds that we are a new person at each successive moment in time, open individualism argues that our sense of unchanging personal identity arises from the being that animates our consciousness. In open individualism, this being or entity does not change through time, instead acting as an unchanging force breathing life into the consciousness of every human. The molecules of our brains still change from moment to moment, but the underlying source of our personal identity never changes. For this reason, we have an intuitive belief that we are the same person throughout our entire lives.

Second, open individualism overcomes the ship of Theseus paradox. Unlike closed individualism, which has trouble explaining why we believe we have the same personal identity we had when we were babies, open individualism again argues that the being animating our minds does not change. Our physical brains do change, but as our consciousness resides within the being that animates our minds, we are the same being from the moment of our birth until our death, and we need explain no paradox. Put another way, open individualism resolves the ship of Theseus paradox by proposing that while it may seem that we are constantly changing, we are in truth eternally unchanging.

Open Individualism And The Afterlife

If the open individualism view of personal identity best explains reality, then life after death becomes absolutely assured. While your existence may seem to consist solely of your mind and body, your consciousness actually resides within an unchanging being. What you think of as your personal identity exists as an illusion, merely a few pages in a novel, brought to life by the force that brings all identities to life.

When you die, it may seem as though your consciousness ceases to exist. While the thoughts and memories attached to your particular identity may disappear, the entity animating all consciousness continues to exist. If every single human consciousness is really just the projection of one being, then when any individual person dies, the animating force of his or her consciousness remains within that being. To go even further, as the being breathes consciousness into every person, when one person dies, his or her consciousness continues to exist within every other conscious human through the existence of the eternal being. As long as the entity that animates us all still exists, then the animating force of your consciousness still exists—even after you die.

Returning to the library analogy, suppose one of the books on the shelf appears old and worn out, with rips and missing pages making the text difficult to read. Such a book would likely be thrown away, or more dramatically, fall apart in the reader's hands when she tries to pick it up. While the story in that book would no longer be legible, the reader—the one who brings the pages to life in his or her mind—still exists. In fact, the reader will continue wandering the aisles, randomly picking up other books. We may be saddened that the story in that one book can no longer be read, but then again, the book consisted solely of some ink placed in a pattern on some paper—the reader, the animating force of the story, still remains.

Similarly, we may be sad when a friend or loved one dies, or contemplating our own mortality, but in the view of open individualism, death results in the loss of only one brain. The being providing the consciousness for that brain still remains, animating all the other brains of all the other humans still alive.

Relationship To Other Philosophies

The basic concepts on which open individualism rest shares similarities with philosophical and religious ideas going back centuries. As Daniel Kolak wrote in his book on open individualism, "[v]ariations on this theme have been voiced periodically throughout the ages, from the Upanishads in the Far East, Averroës in the Middle East, down to Josiah Royce."

The open individualism view was also adopted by the famous physicist and mathematician Freeman

Dyson, who referred to the idea as "Cosmic Unity." To be frank, I would bet that almost everyone who has stayed up until three in the morning discussing deep philosophical questions with friends has experienced the light-headed warmth coming from the thought that we're all one, and that the boundaries that appear to so completely divide us are surprisingly arbitrary. Of course, most of us dismiss the idea in the morning. Perhaps, though, we shouldn't be so quick to reject such an interesting and philosophically coherent view of consciousness.

Regardless of our late-night ramblings, the open individualism idea also intersects in interesting ways with ethics. In fact, one of the primary motivations for Kolak to write a book on open individualism was his interest in how it applied to ethical questions. The crux of the ethical issue follows from the assumption that all our personal identities arise from the same animating force. If we are all one being, all one consciousness separated by illusory personal identities, then if I hurt you, I am also hurting myself. In fact, anytime anyone anywhere feels pain or embarrassment or anxiety, you too have those feelings. On the other hand, anytime anyone anywhere experiences joy or gratitude, you also share in those sensation.

Clearly, the open individualism view provides an extremely strong incentive to reduce suffering everywhere in the world, because to do so will reduce your own suffering. As Dyson wrote in describing his view of Cosmic Unity, "[t]here is no problem of injustice because your sufferings are also mine. There will be no problem of war as soon as you understand that in killing me you are only killing yourself."[5]

But What Exactly Animates Our Minds?

The primary objection I raised to the closed individualism view of personal identity was that it could not explain the ship of Theseus paradox with regard to consciousness. If the conscious mind changes with each new thought, then what moves through time to connect that consciousness in a way that makes it feel like a single personal identity? Open individualism solves this paradox by stating that an unchanging being or entity produces our personal identity, thereby overcoming the paradox. Unfortunately, while this may solve the ship of Theseus paradox, it does so by creating an even bigger problem: Instead of an unknown connection between conscious states creating a unified personal identity, open individualism suggests some ethereal being, pervading all our minds, connecting us all. Where did this being come from? Why has no scientific experiment ever found a trace of it?

Obviously, one answer could be that this being is God. In a book with the word "atheist" in the title, though, this answer does not exactly suffice. Another answer could be that this being is not really a being at all, but a force that conforms to the known laws of physics. I will admit that in this chapter I have purposely anthropomorphized whatever supposed substance or force potentially connects all our conscious minds. I did this in an attempt to make it better fit within the analogy of a person wandering among the stacks of books in a library. The being, however, may not be a being at all, but instead a physical phenomenon that arises out of quantum mechanics or the curvature of space-time. In fact, in developing the idea of open individualism, Kolak does not anthropomorphize whatever connects us; he simply calls it "Consciousness."

If a physical force does animate our conscious minds, that would actually help in sinking the ship of Theseus paradox. Consider if the animating force was instead some ethereal being, walking among humans, choosing which brains to enter like picking up a book. Such a being must surely change through time. If the being changes, then we are back to the ship of Theseus paradox. However, if consciousness arises through the actions of a physical force, then it would never change, and the ship of Theseus paradox would be vanquished.

To see this more clearly, consider the force of gravity. Gravity causes all kinds of objects to fall to the ground, but we do not think of gravity as changing. Instead, we consider gravity to be an unchanging physical force pervading the universe. While gravity may act on many different objects, gravity itself never changes. Similarly, there may exist a physical force that pervades the universe that has the effect of creating consciousness within each human brain. The thoughts within that consciousness may change constantly, but the force itself would never change. In this way, the changing consciousness we experience comes from an unchanging physical force, and the ship of Theseus problem has been solved. More importantly, the force would exist for eternity, meaning that the essence of our consciousness would also exist for eternity.

Regrettably, even if we assume that whatever animates our consciousness is a physical force, we must still admit that there currently exists no scientific evidence for such a force. There also exists no plausible explanation for how this force results in a single unitary identity. Neuroscience appears to very clearly support the hypothesis that consciousness arises out of the structure of the brain. I know of no experiment showing that changes in one brain or consciousness immediately affect the brain or consciousness of a person thousands of miles away. In other words, each one of your feelings does not appear to be instantaneously shared with every other person on the planet. Consequently, even though we are in the philosophical section of this book, we must still consider that no scientific evidence currently exists showing that all consciousness arises from a single being or force.

A Nice Day For Sailing

Open individualism appears to solve both the ship of Theseus paradox and the intuitive feeling that our personal identity remains the same through time. In doing so, however, open individualism creates entirely new problems. Primarily, open individualism requires us to assume the existence of a previously unknown force or being that animates every human mind on Earth. While open individualism remains an interesting philosophical idea, and one very much worth considering, so far, there simply is no evidence that it is true.

Until such evidence arises, we will have to make do with closed individualism or empty individualism. At least at this point in our understanding of the universe, we probably shouldn't rely on open individualism for the afterlife. It looks as though Theseus's ship will need to remain in the Athenian harbor for at least a bit longer.

CHAPTER 7

A SOUL WITHOUT A GOD

After the last chapter, if you are feeling a bit tired of the ancient Greeks and their head-scratching paradoxes, I regret to inform you that this chapter begins with a return to that particular civilization. This time, imagine the ancient Greek gods sitting atop Mt. Olympus, squabbling, making love and war, and generally acting as petty and spiteful as most humans. Now imagine the poets and playwrights concocting the stories about those gods. The storytellers would certainly reason that if the gods act like us in almost every other way, then just as human beings must breathe air to survive, the gods must also breathe something to survive. Breathing the same air as people, though, would be much too coarse and undivine for a group of celestial creatures who enjoy tormenting mortal humans whenever possible. As a result, the ancient poets and playwrights devised something much more magnificent to for the gods to breathe, furnished by the god Aether.

The god Aether has many different origin stories, but in one story he is the son of Chaos and Darkness. Perhaps when you have Chaos and Darkness for parents, you rebel by filling the world with buoyancy and light. Aether did just this by creating a pure, translucent type of air, worthy of the divine. This air was also called aether, and it existed above the terrestrial realm, filling the universe. Consequently, the gods on Mt. Olympus had something to breathe, allowing their squabbling to continue, and we have a label that has come to hold a variety of scientifically important meanings.

The idea that there was some invisible substance filling all of space became a crucial one for scientists beginning in the seventeenth century. In 1678, the Dutch physicist, mathematician, and astronomer Christiaan Huygens (see Figure 7) proposed that light acts as a wave. Before then it had been widely thought that light consisted of particles (of course, as Chapter 3 describes, experiments hundreds of years later would show that light exists as both particles and waves at the same time). Huygens developed his wave theory in part because it helped explain observable refraction patterns produced by light.

Figure 7. An engraving of Christiaan Huygens made between 1684 and 1687. Huygens was one of the first scientists to suggest that an invisible aether filled all empty space. Public domain.

The problem with the wave theory seemed to be that there was nothing to propagate the wave. A wave in the ocean propagates through the water and a sound wave propagates through air. Light, though, can travel through space—such as from the sun to Earth—even though there is no air or water in space to propagate it. The answer Huygens and others proposed was our friend the aether. They hypothesized that light travels in waves through the aether just as sound waves travel through air. For the hypothesis to work, though, aether, unlike air, had to fill all space throughout the entire universe. Even though no one could see the aether, or test that it was there, for the next two hundred years scientists widely believed aether filled the universe. Not until Albert Michelson and Edward Morley developed precise enough optical equipment, in 1887, could a test of the aether theory be performed.

In the Michelson-Morley experiment, the two scientists compared the speed of light in perpendicular directions. If aether existed, then the motion of Earth would cause the aether to move in certain directions, causing aether winds. Light waves traveling through those aether winds should move at different speeds depending on the direction of the wind. The Michelson-Morley experiment, however, found that the speed of light did not differ depending on the direction of the light waves. The experiment thereby provided overwhelming evidence that aether does not fill the universe. (As an aside, besides demonstrating the lack of aether, the Michelson-Morley experiment was also important in motivating Albert Einstein to develop his theory of special relativity.)

Astonishingly, the death knell for the aether hypothesis provided by the Michelson-Morley experiment may have been premature. The empty vacuum of space turns out not to be empty at all. According to the theories of quantum mechanics, empty space constantly produces particle-antiparticle pairs. These particle-antiparticle pairs pop into existence and then quickly annihilate each other, popping out of existence. Take just a moment to ponder that the universe can create particles out of completely empty space. If after popping into existence out of nothingness, one of the particle pairs happens to be pulled into a black hole before annihilating its partner, the unmolested particle can fly off into space. As one particle in the particle-antiparticle pair falls into the black hole, allowing the other particle to speed away, it appears as though the black hole is emitting radiation. This "Hawking radiation" was named after the physicist Stephen Hawking who proposed the phenomenon in 1974. Before you conclude that these supposed particles are the made-up suppositions of theoretical physicists, consider that even experiments conducted in labs on Earth provide strong evidence for the phenomenon of particle-antiparticle pairs popping into existence out of empty space.

The vacuum of space does not only produce particles, however—it also produces energy. In fact, the energy produced by empty space may be the "dark energy" causing the accelerating expansion of the universe. As another aside, if someone tries to argue to you that the existence of the universe proves the existence of God—after all, they may say, how could the universe exist without someone to create it—simply point out that empty space constantly produces particles and energy, and the universe exploding into existence out of nothingness seems more likely than not.

Returning to the quantum world, what may seem like the empty vacuum of space actually has particles and energy permeating throughout. If one were being a bit cheeky, one might even call the particles and energy that fill empty space aether. In fact, the physicist and Nobel Laureate Robert Laughlin wrote in 2005, "studies with large particle accelerators have now led us to understand that space is more like a piece of window glass than ideal Newtonian emptiness. It is filled with 'stuff' that is normally transparent but can be made visible by hitting it sufficiently hard to knock out a part. The modern concept of the vacuum of space, confirmed every day by experiment, is a relativistic [a]ether. But we do not call it this because it is taboo." Perhaps the gods sitting atop Mt. Olympus have something to breathe after all.

I bring this intrusion of science into the philosophical section of the book because it happens to provide a useful analogy. Aether began its existence as a substance created by a god so that other gods would have something to breathe. The aether then became a scientifically accepted hypothesis, existing to explain how waves of light could propagate through empty space. Science then did away with the idea of the aether, claiming that its existence was not necessary to explain known phenomena. Finally, a new understanding of the natural world suggests that the aether may exist, although in a different form than anyone had considered in the past.

I hope to suggest in this chapter that the timeline of the acceptance, dismissal, and potential acceptance of the aether may apply to the concept of the human soul. Originally, people assumed the aether could only exist if created by a god, but now some scientists believe the aether may exist as a fundamental principle of the universe. Similarly, while it may seem the human soul could only derive from the hand of a god, perhaps the soul also exists as a fundamental principle of the universe. Indeed, while the aether may pervade the universe, the soul may pervade the body. To begin this examination, I start with a brief survey of the human soul.

A Quick Tour Of The Soul

The vast majority of human cultures contain some form of belief in an incorporeal soul separate from the physical body. Most people in prehistoric societies likely believed in the concept of the soul, although the lack of writing makes it a tad difficult to know for sure. We do know that the ancient Egyptians believed that the soul was composed of many different parts, such as the identity, spiritual body, personality, and form. After death, if priests performed the correct rituals, the different components of the soul would reunite in the afterlife. The beliefs of the ancient Egyptians closely mirror the Taoist beliefs originating in fourth century BCE China. In Taoism, the individual again has several souls, with the earthly soul disappearing with death, while the spiritual soul attains immortality.

In early Judaism, the soul was not considered separate from the body. The first Jewish religious thinkers held that God breathed the soul into the body, allowing the body to live, but that the body and soul were not separate—the death of the one meant the death of the other. Later Jewish philosophers, however, developed the idea that the soul consists of five components that describe the entirety of the spirit. After the death of the body, according to these later thinkers, the soul would continue to exist.

As relatively newer religions became more strongly monotheistic, their views of the soul also changed. Islam and Christianity are both monotheistic and share similar views of the soul. Both religions hold that each person consists of a mortal body and a single indivisible immortal soul attached to that body. When the mortal body dies, the soul does not die, but continues to exist for eternity.

All these conceptions of the soul have several properties in common. First, the soul is incorporeal and resides within (or somehow attaches itself to) the physical body. Second, the soul, whether composed of several different components or only one indivisible substance, describes the entirety of a person's individuality and consciousness. Third, after the death of the physical body, the soul continues to exist.

This third property obviously inspires the most interest. In some religions, the soul that continues to exist after death consists of only the reasoning portion of the mind that has just died. In many other religions, though, the soul that continues after death contains the entire memory, personality, and consciousness of the mind that has just perished.

Before moving on to the next section, I should point out that I have purposefully left out the Buddhist understanding of the soul. In some Buddhist teachings individuals have souls, but those souls do not survive the death of the physical body. I have refrained from a discussion of Buddhism in this section as I intend to briefly take up the subject in the next chapter.

Surveys Of Belief

While a tour of ancient religious dogma may be interesting, it doesn't really say much about what people currently believe about the soul. Fortunately, in 2018 the Pew Research Center conducted a survey of religious beliefs in fifteen Western European countries. Across the fifteen countries, 27 percent of the people interviewed believed in God as described in the Bible. An additional 38 percent did not believe in the God from the Bible but did believe in a higher power. Unsurprisingly, the vast majority of those who said they believed in the God of the Bible or a higher power also believed they had a soul.

Then the results became much more interesting. A full 26 percent of those interviewed stated that they did not believe in God or any higher power. Amazingly, of those individuals, a large percentage also said they believed they had a soul. In Sweden, 14 percent of nonbelievers said they thought they had a soul. In the United Kingdom the number was 22 percent. Finally, in the Netherlands, the number of people who did not believe in God or a higher power but did believe that they had a soul was an astonishing 43 percent.

Before thinking that these results are confined to European countries and European cultures, consider a 2017 Pew Research Center survey of US beliefs. While the questions were different and cannot be directly compared, the results hint at similar findings. When asked, "Do you believe in God, or not," 19 percent of Americans answered no. The Pew survey then dug a bit deeper. For those Americans who described themselves as agnostics, Pew found that 62 percent stated they believed in a spiritual force. Most surprising of all, among those Americans who described themselves as atheists, 18 percent stated they believed in a spiritual force in the universe.

While belief in a spiritual force does not automatically translate to belief in a soul, the likelihood of the two beliefs coinciding seems high. The results from the surveys of religious convictions in Western Europe and the US show that a large percentage of people do not believe in God or any kind of higher spiritual power, but do believe they have souls separate from their bodies.

What are we to make of a belief that at first seems so contradictory? How can a person believe in a soul separate from his body, but not believe in a god who stuck it there? The remainder of this chapter will be devoted to arguing that holding these two seemingly contradictory beliefs at the same time isn't as paradoxical as it first appears. In fact, belief in the human soul but not God is philosophically justifiable. Whether one then goes on to hold that the soul truly does exist, and continues to exist after the physical body dies, remains a personal decision each one of us must make on our own.

Arguments For The Soul

There are several arguments for the existence of the soul, but I'll focus on the three main arguments that don't require any reference to a god. The first argument arises out of a failure—the failure of science to convincingly explain human consciousness. Given that modern science seems capable of explaining everything else in the universe, why does it fail at illuminating consciousness? Perhaps the answer may be found by proposing that something beyond physical phenomena acts as the spark for consciousness.

The second argument for the soul derives from an intuitive belief many people hold about themselves— that they are more than their physical bodies. Humans tend to be wrong about a lot of stuff, but perhaps we should give some credence to a belief so widely held by so many people.

The third and final argument stems from the unexplainable nature of a very old but continually recurring story—the out-of-body experience. A true out-of-body experience would almost certainly be proof of the soul.

Some of these arguments hold up better under scrutiny than others (don't worry, I'll cast plenty of doubt on out-of-body experiences). However, each argument deserves its own consideration, and should be viewed within the larger context provided by the other two arguments. The following sections tackle these three arguments in turn.

First Argument: Consciousness Requires A Soul

In several of the previous chapters in this book, I confidently asserted that neuroscientists will eventually understand consciousness well enough to allow them to program computers to simulate the human brain. A small group of scientists and philosophers aren't so sure. The philosopher John Searle argued that consciousness depends on the biology of cells, writing that consciousness, "is a biological phenomenon, and it is as likely to be as causally dependent on the specific biochemistry of its origins as lactation, photosynthesis, or any other biological phenomena. No one would suppose that we could produce milk and sugar by running a computer simulation of the formal sequences in lactation and photosynthesis."[6] According to Searle, a computer may be able to simulate the steps for consciousness, but that does not mean the computer actually creates consciousness.

Some thinkers extend this argument even further. First assume, as Searle argues, that a computer cannot truly simulate a biological process such as photosynthesis because the steps require biochemical reactions to proceed (i.e., a computer cannot output tree sap). If this is true, then why should we assume that biological processes that have no consciousness of their own are able to produce consciousness? Biochemical reactions—such as those occurring in a brain—do not have emotions or ideas, so perhaps they cannot be the source of human consciousness. This is the argument made by the philosopher Richard Swinburne, who puts it much more succinctly as, "atoms do not have thoughts and feelings."[7] This argument is bolstered by remembering that scientists have been seriously studying the biology of the human brain for over one hundred years, but are no closer to explaining consciousness than when they began. How can neuroscience claim to know anything about consciousness if it can't even explain why you hear a voice in your head when you read a sentence in a book?

Maybe there is a reason science has yet to explain consciousness through the laws of physics. Our conscious minds produce so many amazing thoughts and emotions, and direct such intricate and complex actions, that intuitively it seems hard to believe that any scientific explanation reduced to neurons and neurotransmitters could explain the experience of being a thinking human being. Maybe science has yet to explain consciousness because science cannot explain consciousness. Perhaps consciousness requires something beyond the known physical laws in order to exist. As Swinburne wrote, consciousness "cannot be the property of a mere body, a material object. It must be a property of something else connected to a body; and to that something else I shall give the traditional name of soul."[8] If the natural laws of the universe cannot explain consciousness, then maybe consciousness requires the existence of something outside of natural laws—maybe consciousness requires a soul.

Of course, most scientists and philosophers do not believe consciousness requires any explanation beyond the known laws of physics. The most common argument for how consciousness arises out of biological phenomena relies on the concept of emergent properties. An emergent property occurs when an entity made of many individual parts displays a property that none of the individual parts have on their own. In other words, a property of the entity emerges only when the individual parts that make up that entity interact. For example, the shape of a snowflake emerges from the interaction of individual water molecules. All water molecules have the same shape, but when the individual molecules interact in the right conditions, beautiful patterns form. Similarly, some argue that no individual neuron is conscious, but when billions of neurons interact, consciousness emerges.

Consciousness as an emergent property of biological processes is likely correct (if I were a betting man, that is certainly where I would place my money). However, I must point out again that no scientist or philosopher has proposed a satisfactory explanation for how consciousness emerges from the interaction of neurons. Scientists have no problem simulating how millions of water molecules interact to form a snowflake; no such simulation exists to show how consciousness arises from the biology of the brain. Again, perhaps this lack of scientific progress is because consciousness does not arise solely from the biology of the brain.

Not surprisingly, many religious philosophers have used human consciousness as an argument for the existence of God. They make claims similar to the one made just now: Human consciousness seems to be a unique phenomenon that cannot be explained by science, therefore it must be explained by the existence of the soul, and the existence of the soul can only be explained by the existence of God.

Despite what religious thinkers may argue, though, the inability of science to explain consciousness makes a much better case for the existence of the soul than for the existence of God. Based on our own personal experience, we know and understand what it means to be conscious. If physical laws cannot explain that experience, then it makes sense to look beyond those laws at the possibility of a soul. Where souls come from becomes the next logical question. The origin of the soul, however, has many possible answers, with God being fairly low down on the list. The question of where souls come from will be taken up later in the chapter; for now it suffices to assert that we have no need to rely on an omnipotent and omniscient God to create them. As a consequence, the existence of a soul does very little to prove the existence of God. We have the experience of consciousness and may need a soul to explain it; we have no experience of God and therefore no need to assume one.

Second Argument: More Than Just A Body

I have a small telescope that, on clear nights, I like to set up in my backyard. I live in a city, so my skies are never very dark, but I am still able to see planets, galaxies, and globular clusters with my little scope. The objects in my eyepiece may shake and jiggle, and are never very bright, but I am able to see beyond the veil of this planet. I am constantly awed by the thought that the light shining into my telescope took hundreds or thousands of years to reach my eye. When I am looking at a galaxy or nebula, knowing that I am seeing the object as it appeared thousands of years ago, I often feel an expansion of my very being. In that moment I believe without doubt that I am more than just this body and this mind—I feel a connection binding me to the entire universe.

The feeling only lasts for a few seconds, and I tend to snap out of it when I put the telescope away. I would be willing to bet, though, that almost everyone reading this book has had a similar type of experience. At some point, almost all of us feel as though we are part of something larger than ourselves. When such a feeling arises, it seems downright ludicrous to think that we can explain our lives, our very existence, without reference to something beyond us.

Why do so many of us experience this sense of metaphysical grandeur? An evolutionary hypothesis might suggest that a desire to belong to a tribe could be important for human survival, and a feeling of oneness with the universe merely indicates an overactive longing to be part of a clan. A different evolutionary hypothesis may hold that we are primed to assume that even random phenomena are caused by intelligent agents acting with purpose. As a result, perhaps I am so amazed to see light that took thousands of years to reach my eye that I intuitively believe some mystical force beyond the random accumulation of gas into stars caused that light to seek me out. Similar evolutionary arguments have been made for why humans tend to believe in gods.

The evolutionary hypotheses seem insufficient, though. A tendency to believe that random phenomena are acting with purpose, or a desire to belong to a group, may make evolutionary sense; but those supposed evolutionary impulses don't seem to capture the overpowering feeling of oneness with the universe. We shouldn't be too quick to dismiss a sensation felt at least occasionally by almost every human being who has ever lived. Maybe our feelings of mystical oneness accurately reflect something about the universe.

For many people, the most likely explanation for their mystical feelings is a soul separate from the physical body. The existence of such a soul would almost certainly share in the bonds of the universe in a way in which the body does not. Any feelings of oneness with the universe would flow naturally from the connection of the soul to the links connecting all living things.

There are of course very good arguments against using a mystical experience as evidence for the existence of the soul. We may feel as though we have a soul, but humans are notoriously unreliable when we use our feelings to understand the universe. For example, it simply feels true that the earth stays motionless while the sun moves across the sky—maybe even dragged by a chariot! But just because something feels true does not make it true. Similarly, just because we feel that we are more than our physical bodies does not provide solid evidence for the soul. Additionally, no scientific experiment has found any evidence that a mystical sensation comes from anything other than the very real neurons packed inside our brains. Nonetheless, an experience of oneness, shared by so many and as yet unexplained, provides at least the slightest additional bit of evidence for the existence of a human soul.

Third Argument: Out-Of-Body Experiences

We have likely all read the stories of a patient whose heart stops beating on the operating table, often spending several minutes clinically dead before being resuscitated by doctors. Upon awakening, the patient reports that he felt his consciousness rise up from his physical body. Occasionally, the patient describes remaining in the room, watching the doctors struggle to bring life back to his body; other times he recounts floating into a white light and reuniting with relatives who had died years earlier.

Clearly, if it could be proven that consciousness rises out of the physical body at death, out-of-body experiences would represent extremely strong evidence for the existence of the soul. A continuation of the conscious mind after the physical death of the body, along with that consciousness separating spatially from the body, could only occur if humans had some sort of incorporeal appendage attached to the brain.

Similar to the metaphysical feeling of oneness described in the previous section, out-of-body experiences are a widespread phenomenon. Doctors have been writing about patients who describe experiencing an out-of-body event since at least the eighteenth century. Additionally, almost every culture in the world has reports of individuals who have had out-of-body experiences while near death. Such a prevalent phenomenon must be taken at least somewhat seriously.

Currently, though, no evidence exists to corroborate the out-of-body experiences as relayed by those who have undergone them. In several emergency rooms, doctors have placed signs above the lights hanging from the ceilings. A person standing on the floor or lying in a bed would not be able to see the signs, as they are hidden behind the lights. Only a soul floating above the lights, looking down on its former body, would be able to see the writing on the signs. So far, no one has had an out-of-body experience and been able to report what is displayed on the signs. While this certainly does not prove that out-of-body experiences never occur, it does illustrate how there is currently no proof for them either. At this point in time, doctors and scientists have simply found no independent evidence for any out-of-body experience.

As with sensations of oneness with the universe, we must be careful in the conclusions we draw. We cannot simply accept that the widespread occurrence of out-of-body experiences provides evidence for a soul separate from the body. On the other hand, we also cannot simply accept that we know precisely what causes out-of-body experiences. We should continue to probe these experiences to try and understand just what they do tell us about ourselves and about the universe.

What Do The Arguments Prove?

The three arguments outlined above suggest that maybe, just maybe, consciousness requires the existence of something beyond the known laws of physics. Each one of the three arguments should be understood as helping to prop up the other two. Almost every one of us has had the feeling that we are a small part of something much larger than ourselves. On occasion, some people experience this feeling so strongly that they alter the entire course of their lives in response. Additionally, in the trauma of a near-death experience, the feeling of being part of something larger may manifest itself as an out-of-body experience. Similar to how almost all of us occasionally experience a mystical sense of oneness, many people across time and cultures have had out-of-body experiences—most of them reporting the sensation of their conscious minds leaving their physical bodies. The mystical sensation and the out-of-body experience merge with the inability of science to adequately explain consciousness to suggest that science *cannot* adequately explain consciousness. If science cannot explain consciousness, and personal experience evokes a strong suspicion that consciousness relies on more than just the physical matter of the brain, then we must consider the possibility of the human soul. For a problem as hard to solve as consciousness, we should rule nothing out.

Do these three arguments prove that the soul exists? Of course not. Perhaps, though, they hint that something beyond the purely material world exists to help animate our minds. Perhaps that something is indeed the soul.

A Soul Of The Gaps

Of the three arguments in the previous sections, the contention that the soul exists because science has not yet explained consciousness appears to be the strongest.

However, such an argument opens up a critique similar to those leveled against philosophers arguing for the existence of God. This critique usually goes by the name of "God of the gaps."

The God of the gaps critique comes from philosophers trying to prove the existence of the divine entity. A thousand years ago a Christian philosopher needed only point to the presence of the universe, the earth, animals, plants, and humans, to convincingly argue for the existence of God. At that point in time, no serious alternative theory could explain why the universe existed, or how creatures as complex as humans came to be. A thousand years ago, belief in the existence of God was perhaps even a rational belief.

The history of science, though, has been a history of reducing such complex phenomena to understandable and testable theories. Scientists would eventually show that the existence of mountains or oceans or rivers could be explained by geological phenomena, meaning that there was no need to invoke God to explain why mountains existed or why earthquakes occurred. Religious philosophers would often accept that natural laws explained those *particular* phenomena, but that God was needed to explain anything more complex, such as a tree or a horse. As science continued to advance, though, researchers formulated testable theories to explain the existence of plants and animals. Reluctantly, most religious philosophers accepted that God may not be needed to explain plant and animal evolution, but He was surely necessary to explain the existence of the universe. Then scientists laid out the big bang theory, and suddenly God wasn't even necessary to explain the universe.

Right now, Christian philosophers trying to find phenomena that science hasn't explained are more or less left with the origin of the big bang and human consciousness. A philosopher trying to prove the existence of God can only point to these two phenomena as possible evidence for the hand of the divine. As science advances, God rules over an ever-diminishing realm.

Many Christian philosophers have rejected this idea of a God who exists only to explain the smaller and smaller gaps in human knowledge. In other words, they reject a God of the gaps. These philosophers argue that God must be invoked to explain all observable phenomena, not just those few occurrences science cannot yet fully describe.

Some people reading this chapter will launch the same critique at the idea of a soul without a god. I have argued that the greatest evidence for the soul comes from the fact that scientists do not yet have a satisfactory explanation for human consciousness. Hundreds of years ago many people believed that souls were the animators of all human thought and emotion, and our brains simply existed to help cool our blood. We now understand the importance of neurons and neurotransmitters in producing thoughts and regulating our bodies. At best, we only need the soul to explain that final spark that allows for consciousness. Put another way, over the last few hundred years, the human soul has already become a soul of the gaps. If neuroscientists ever formulate a satisfactory theory of consciousness, or computer scientists reproduce consciousness in a computer, then suddenly the gap closes, and we no longer need a soul.

At this point in time, though, science has yet to satisfactorily explain consciousness. The gap still exists and may be one of the few gaps scientists never close. While there still remains a gap, we must consider a soul to fill it.

What Happens To The Soul When The Body Dies?

Most religions that teach that humans have souls also teach that God determines what happens to those souls after the body dies. God doesn't just let souls float around the universe for the rest of eternity, He puts them into some version of heaven or hell or underworld. If you believe God created your soul, it only makes sense you would also believe He has a plan for what to do with it after your physical body dies.

If God does not exist, though, and no divine being organizes where to put all those souls after their corresponding bodies die, then what exactly happens to them? Without a God, where do disembodied souls go?

With no God, we certainly shouldn't expect souls to go to what we traditionally think of as heaven. While this might be disappointing, at least it also means there is no chance that your soul will end up suffering for eternity in hell. Much more likely than heaven or hell, the death of the body would release the soul into the seemingly empty space of the universe. Perhaps each soul connects with the dark energy of the universe, somehow joining with the aether.

What would such an afterlife be like? I must admit that I have no clue. Maybe the conscious thoughts and memories of the person would continue with the soul as it departs the body, and would float throughout the universe, wherever it desired, for the rest of time. Maybe the soul would only retain some of the thoughts and memories of the body, and that partial consciousness would drift randomly — in the emptiness of space one moment, buffeted by the heat and energy of a star the next. We have no reason to assume that, without a god purposefully organizing a place for souls that have left their bodies, being a soul without a body would be a pleasant experience. We may each have a soul that exists after we die, but we may come to wish that we didn't.

I realize this entire section probably seems like wondering how many angels can fit on the head of a pin. We have no proof for the existence of the soul, so wondering about what happens to the soul after we die comes off as premature at best. On the other hand, if we can speculate about the existence of the soul, we should certainly feel free to speculate about what happens to the soul after it stops being housed in a material body. The more essential question, and the one I have purposefully left until late in the chapter, is where in the universe souls come from in the first place?

If God Does Not Exist, Where Do Souls Come From?

If we assume God exists, then the problem of where the human soul comes from requires no explanation— God creates each soul and plunks it into a body. As I've already pointed out once or twice, though, this book begins with the assumption that God does not exist. So where do souls come from if God does not create them?

At first glance, the need to answer this question seems essential. After all, a soul that plays a role in consciousness and exists after death must certainly have been designed by someone. But after a bit of reflection, perhaps the origin of the soul should be of less concern. After all, we accept that Earth, the solar system, and even the universe itself are the results of natural laws that had no intelligent creator. If the soul exists, we have no reason to presume it requires a designer. A soul may exist under laws that simply are not yet understood by humans. The quantum mind described in Chapter 4, or the animating force of open individualism described in Chapter 6, could both easily fit within the definition of the soul in this chapter. To return to the aether at the beginning of this chapter, perhaps souls simply pop into existence, like particles in the vacuum of space.

The problem with supposing that the soul springs into being through physical processes comes from the fact that no evidence exists of physical processes giving rise to anything even remotely resembling a soul. As the physicist Sean Carroll has written, we have no experimental evidence for "spirit particles" that interact with atoms. If such spirit particles did exist, scientists likely would have detected them by now.

An Incorporeal Whisper

Once again, we are left with only the merest hints and whispers of a soul. Many people unexpectedly encounter the sensation that they are more than their physical body, whether when near death or merely looking up at the stars. On top of that, after more than a century of close study, scientists have yet to explain consciousness.

Do these intimations of the human soul overcome a lack of physical evidence for such a soul? Do they overcome the lack of meaningful theories for how the soul functions or where it comes from? At this point, for those surveyed by the Pew Research Center who do not believe in God but do believe in a spiritual force, the slimmest possibility that the soul exists will have to be enough.

CHAPTER 8

REINCARNATION AND THE DETERMINISTIC UNIVERSE

I f you have ever had the wearying feeling that you've seen it all and done it all, you may be more correct than you think. Buddhist philosophy teaches that humans are caught in an endless cycle of death and rebirth called Samsara. Every time a person dies, he or she quickly becomes reincarnated in a different physical form. This reincarnation may not result in the person being reborn as another human being, though, but instead as an animal or even in some other realm of existence (see Figure 8). In Buddhist thought, being reincarnated as a human requires doing good acts while alive, and thereby having good karma.

Figure 8. A traditional Tibetan mural depicting the six realms of Samsara in which a person may be reborn after death. Stephen Shephard, CC BY-SA.

On the other hand, being reincarnated as an animal results from doing bad acts while alive and having bad karma.

The rebirth doctrine in Buddhism has a bit of a problem, however, because it seems to conflict with another important Buddhist doctrine. Buddhist philosophy holds that there is no permanent self or soul, and no continuation of an individual's memory after death. Each time you are reincarnated, you do not remember anything about your past lives. But if the self and the soul are not permanent, then what exactly is being reincarnated?

As may be expected for such an important question within Buddhism, there are several different answers that have arisen from different Buddhist schools of thought. Some schools hold that consciousness does indeed move from body to body during the Samsara cycle of death and rebirth. Under this doctrine, the memories of previous lives remain after reincarnation, and may even be recovered during meditation. Other schools, though, argue that only an inexpressible self, called *avacya*, achieves rebirth from one life to the next. Unfortunately, this inexpressible self does not contain the consciousness or memories of past lives.

All schools of Buddhist thought, however, believe in the goal of attaining nirvana. Nirvana means escape from the cycle of death and rebirth described by the Samsara. A person attains nirvana by following the path of Buddhist teachings and learning to extinguish all desire. Once again, there are different schools of thought within Buddhism on what exactly attaining nirvana means. Some schools teach that nirvana means attaining a transcendent consciousness that exists beyond space and time. Other schools hold that because Buddhism teaches that humans have no permanent self or soul, attaining nirvana means escaping the cycle of death and rebirth to truly become nothingness—no desire, no pain, no thought, no self.

Before we reach nirvana, though, I want to return to the idea that the conscious mind does not become reincarnated, only the *avacya*—the inexpressible self—achieves rebirth. If nothing that you can identify as yourself, no thoughts or memories, achieves reincarnation, have you really been reborn? Some Buddhist thinkers have argued that the inexpressible self becomes reincarnated in the way that our actions and thoughts leave behind impressions on all those we have influenced or interacted with while we were alive. This comes a bit too close to the old cliché that as long as your loved ones remember you, you are not truly dead. Such a version of reincarnation would be rebirth in only the most superficial of ways.

But thinking about reincarnation of the inexpressible self a bit differently may reveal it to be more than just a cliché. If we consider reincarnation to be understood as every action you have taken in your life reverberating across the planet for the rest of time, then perhaps it is a bit more substantial. Reincarnation of the inexpressible self may mean that life after death exists in the way that your thoughts and actions continue to influence every other life-form on Earth after you die. That influence may even continue until the end of time, or at least until no more life exists anywhere on Earth—that is, until nirvana. To explore this version of the afterlife, we need to first take a quick tour of determinism and free will.

Determinism

The philosophy of determinism holds that every event in the universe has been determined entirely by previous events. This means that if you happen to know all the elements and forces that are about to act on a certain event, you could predict with absolute certainty the outcome of that event. As an example, in your everyday life you know that when you flip a coin it has a 50 percent chance of landing heads up, and a 50 percent chance of landing tails up. You don't know until you flip the coin which side will land facing up. Under determinism, though, if you know all the elements and forces acting upon the coin, you would be able to predict with 100 percent certainty how the coin would land

While being able to predict the outcome of a coin toss might come in handy when deciding on who has to make the bed, the real importance of determinism lies in what it can tell us about the universe. Imagine that you were somehow able to know the exact location and velocity of every single particle in the universe a millisecond after the big bang. If the universe is deterministic, then knowing the location and velocity of each particle right after the big bang would allow you to predict the location and velocity of each particle a second later. Knowing this information would allow you to predict everything about those particles a second after that, and on and on. This means that you could state with absolute certainty everything that is about to happen in the universe right now, and a minute from now, and a million years from now. Moreover, if you were to rewind the universe to the big bang and then let it go forward, the exact same version of events would occur again. No matter how many times you rewound the universe, an identical universe to this one would occur each time. To put this another way, in a deterministic universe, the events that happened a millisecond after the big bang have determined every other event in the entire universe up until now, and will continue to determine every event until the end of time.

Many philosophers throughout history have believed in determinism; but philosophers being philosophers, many have also believed in the exact opposite. Philosophers call the opposite hypothesis indeterminism. Indeterminism holds that all events are probabilistic, and the most you can know is the probability of one event or another happening. In this view, if you were to know the exact location and velocity of every particle in the universe a bit after the big bang, you could only give vanishingly small probabilities of what will happen in the universe a second from now. Additionally, under indeterminism, if you were to rewind the universe several times and let it go forward, you would get completely different universes each time.

The Physics Of Determinism

Once again, physics must invade the philosophy section of the book. The quantum world described in Chapter 4 seems to rule in favor of indeterminism and against determinism. Recall that under the standard interpretation of quantum mechanics, all particles have wave functions. The wave function for a given particle gives the probabilities for the position of that particle in space. When a scientist measures a particle's position, the wave function collapses, and the scientist finds the particle at only one location in space. Consequently, at the quantum level the universe appears fundamentally random.

A different example may help make the idea slightly more intuitive. Suppose you happen to have a pound of plutonium-244 lying around your house. As far as we know, every single atom of plutonium-244 in the universe is completely identical to every other atom of plutonium-244. (The same holds true for all other atoms as well—for instance, no scientific test can distinguish between one atom of carbon-12 and another atom of carbon-12.) Now suppose you left that lump of plutonium-244 sitting in your house for 80.8 million years. When you looked at the lump again, you would find that half the plutonium-244 atoms had radioactively decayed while half were still plutonium atoms. The question becomes, how could determinism possibly account for the seemingly random nature of radioactive decay? All the plutonium-244 particles started off as identical, but during those 80.8 million years, half the atoms decayed and half did not. Determinism does not appear to have any way of predicting which particles will radioactively decay and which will not—it seems to be just random luck.

Randomness arising out of an indeterministic universe must be the only answer.

The randomness of the quantum world puts determinism in serious doubt. Surprisingly, a random universe and a slightly limited form of determinism may still coexist peacefully in the guise of adequate determinism.

Adequate Determinism

Adequate determinism proposes that while the universe may not be truly deterministic, it may be close enough that for humans (and butterflies and amoebas and all other living things), it may as well be deterministic. To support this claim, adequate determinism argues that while quantum indeterminacy causes events to be random at the quantum scale, those random events average out at larger scales. Quantum particles may exhibit truly random behavior, but because there are so many of them in even the smallest bit of living matter, the randomness of individual particles cancel each other out and becomes the predictable laws of classical physics.

To understand this idea better, let's grab the coin from earlier in the chapter. Assume again that when flipped, the coin has a 50 percent chance of landing heads up and a 50 percent chance of landing tails up. If you flip the coin two times, you wouldn't be surprised if the coin landed heads up once and tails up once. However, you also wouldn't be surprised if the coin landed heads up two times in a row or tails up two times in a row. But consider how surprised you would be if you flipped the coin ten times and all ten times it landed heads up. If you flipped the coin a thousand times and it landed tails up every time you would probably begin to question the laws of the universe (or maybe begin to think that gods are real and you must be one of them). This suggests that while the outcome of each individual flip of the coin is random, if we repeat the process millions or billions of times we can feel confident that almost exactly 50 percent of the coin flips will land heads up, and almost exactly 50 percent will land tails up.

The same idea holds for adequate determinism. Over 80.8 million years we have no idea which particles in our pound of plutonium-244 will decay, but we can predict that half will decay, and half will not. We don't need to know exactly which particles will decay to be confident in our prediction. The individual particles of the quantum world display randomness, but there are billions upon billions of particles that make up something as large as a cell, brain, or person. The randomness of all those particles averages out, meaning that the actions of the cell or brain or person appear to be almost entirely deterministic. At a fundamental level the universe may be indeterministic, but at the scale of human beings the universe is adequately deterministic.

Just how deterministic is adequately deterministic? If you were to rewind the universe to the big bang hundreds of times you would still get very different outcomes each time. On the other hand, over shorter time frames, the universe may be adequately deterministic enough to appear fully deterministic. Recall that rewinding the universe to the big bang means going back 13.8 billion years. What if you rewound the universe back only 200,000 years to when modern humans first evolved? Maybe rewinding only 200,000 years would result in almost the exact same events occurring over and over again. In other words, the universe may be random and indeterministic, but on the short time scale in which modern humans have existed, the universe may be deterministic enough that every event that occurred was destined to occur.

Free Will

While the battle between determinism and indeterminism may seem to matter only to neurotic philosophers, the outcome has important consequences for our understanding of ourselves as human beings. Whether determinism or indeterminism rules the universe may control whether humans have free will or not.

For the purposes of this section, I define free will as the ability to make choices unhindered by the past. The concept of free will is fairly intuitive but let me give a couple of contrasting examples. Consider a very simple computer program that when run, outputs on the screen the words "Hello, World!" When a user runs the program, the program determines the exact outcome produced by the computer—no matter how many times the program is run, the output is always the same. The computer has no choice in its actions and therefore clearly has no free will. Conversely, imagine you are getting dressed in the morning and you have two clean shirts to choose from, a red shirt and a blue shirt. The choice of which shirt to wear appears to rest entirely with you, completely unhindered by anything in the past. Of course, your past actions resulted in you having a red shirt and a blue shirt in front of you, but the choice between those two shirts is entirely yours. In other words, you appear to have free will.

In a deterministic universe, though, the answer to whether you have free will is not so obvious. Under determinism, the events of the past entirely control the events of the future. It may feel as though you are choosing between the red shirt and the blue shirt, but that choice was already made by the state of your brain several seconds before, and the state of your brain several seconds before was determined by the state of your brain several years before, and the state of your brain several years before was determined by events hundreds of thousands of years before you were born. If determinism rules the universe, then every choice you make was predetermined. Like a computer program that completely controls the output on a screen, under determinism, the position and velocity of particles thousands of years ago have controlled every event throughout the entire universe since then. If every choice you have ever made, and every choice you will ever make in the future, have already been decided, then you clearly do not have free will.

An indeterministic universe provides a way for us to reclaim our free will. The random nature of quantum particles under indeterminism means that the events of the past do not directly determine the events of the future. The state of your brain a few seconds before does not determine whether you choose the blue or the red shirt, because the state of your brain from second to second depends in part on the randomness of the quantum world. As a consequence, the choices you make are not wholly determined by the past, and we are justified in our intuitive sense of our own free will.

But even in an indeterministic universe, what kind of free will do we really have? Resting the concept of free will on the randomness of quantum particles feels a bit precarious. Imagine you are having trouble deciding between the red and blue shirts, so you decide to flip a coin—heads for the red shirt and tails for the blue. If the coin lands heads up and you put on the red shirt, did you really make the choice to wear the red shirt, or did the coin make the choice for you? Now imagine you don't flip a coin, and you make a conscious decision to wear the red shirt. That decision was decided in part by the randomness of quantum particles. How does adding up the probabilistic nature of quantum particles become free will?

What about adequate determinism—does it change how we think about free will? Under adequate determinism the universe is indeterministic, but for humans and other living things it may as well be deterministic. Adequate determinism suggests that we humans do have free will because ultimately the universe is indeterministic; however, the extent of our free will is extremely limited, as the recent past almost entirely determines the future. In other words, the past does not completely control the future, but the range of choices we have at any point in time is severely curtailed by previous events. Perhaps adequate determinism fits our intuitive sense of reality the best. We intuitively believe we have free will, and that our choices are under our control. We also intuitively believe that our past choices play a large role in determining our current choices. A universe of adequate determinism that allows us to have free will, but greatly circumscribes that free will, may best explain the universe.

The debate over whether humans have free will or not has been ongoing for thousands of years—I'm certainly not going to resolve it in this chapter. Perhaps whether the universe is deterministic or indeterministic ultimately has little bearing on free will. We can all agree that our brains our composed of molecules, and those molecules are composed of quantum particles. In an indeterministic universe our decisions are controlled by the random nature of quantum particles, while in a deterministic universe our decisions are controlled by the previous interactions of those quantum particles. Either way, the quantum world controls every one of our thoughts and actions, and decrees whether we have true free will or only think we do.

Before leaving free will, I want to quickly examine how it interacts with the block universe hypothesis discussed in Chapter 3. Recall that in a block universe, time does not flow unceasingly in one direction. Instead, the past, present, and future all exist simultaneously. The block universe helps explain how time seems to moves at different rates for different observers depending on velocity and gravity, as well as how the order of events may be different for different observers.

In a block universe, the future already exists—this means that all your future choices have already been made. Put another way, in a block universe, your future choices have been predetermined. This appears to fit quite nicely with determinism. In a deterministic universe, the past determines your choices, so again all your future choices have already been predetermined. As a result of this predetermination, in a deterministic universe you do not truly have free will. There is a very real difference, though, between a deterministic universe and the block universe hypothesis. In a block universe, random events may still determine what happens from one moment to the next, but in the block universe all those moments—past, present, and future—already exist. This means that within a block universe, your choices are predetermined because the future already exists, but at the moment in which you make each of those choices the universe is indeterministic and you have free will. In other words, in a block universe, you have both free will and a predetermined future.

The distinction between a predetermined future with free will and a predetermined future without free will may be incredibly small. The difference, though, has consequences for the reincarnation of the inexpressible self. For the remainder of the chapter I assume that we exist in an adequately deterministic universe, and one that is not a block universe.

Reincarnation

After detours to free will and the quantum world, this chapter can finally turn to the effects of determinism on reincarnation. In a deterministic universe, the events of the past completely determine the events of the future. This means that everything you do now — every action you take, even every thought you have — helps to directly determine events in the future. Even the smallest movements of body or mind interact with the surrounding environment, which in turn interacts with the larger universe. Like throwing the rock from Chapter 5 into a pond, causing waves to ripple out along the water, each action or thought you have causes ripples that spread out for eternity, determining future events.

These ripples, spreading out from each action and thought in your life, may be a path to reincarnation. If the actions of your life deterministically influence events long after your death, then that can only be described as the reincarnation of the inexpressible self. After you die, the events of your life continue to influence the events of the future for the rest of time. Your mind and body are not reincarnated — you do not retain any memories after you die. However, the inexpressible self remains in the universe in the way that the events of your life continue to ripple ever outward, influencing future events for eternity.

Consider again the Buddhist concept of reincarnation. According to the most common Buddhist teachings, while you may be reincarnated when you die, your thoughts and memories do not flow into the next body. Through karma, though, your actions when you are alive affect your newly reincarnated body after you die. A deterministic universe suggests a very similar form of reincarnation. In a deterministic universe, your consciousness does not continue to exist after you die. Your thoughts and actions while you are alive, however, directly influence the thoughts and actions of other living beings long after you are dead. Your inexpressible self becomes reincarnated again and again in all the living beings you directly influence after you die.

Besides considering how our actions influence other living beings after death, we should also contemplate how our physical bodies influence other living beings after we die. After death, the molecules that make up our bodies begin to break down, and the atoms within those molecules return to the environment. Once freed from our bodies, those atoms are again recruited to make up new molecules and new compounds and new living creatures. If the atoms that make up our bodies become incorporated into other living beings after we die, then we are again influencing life after death. Becoming part of other living creatures may represent another form of reincarnation of the inexpressible self.

Interestingly, you are constantly shedding parts of your body when you are alive—skin cells, intestinal cells, etc. The atoms that make up those cells are very likely to find their way into other living beings. To think of this process in another way, even when you are alive you are being constantly reincarnated. Even more amazingly, whenever you eat or take in a breath of air, you are bringing atoms from the environment into your body. Once inside of you, some of those atoms become incorporated into the structure of your body. Many of those atoms were previously part of a living being (e.g., the chicken meat you eat, or the broccoli florets you consume, come from formerly living animals and plants). This means that every time you take a bite of food, and even every time you take a breath of air, you are reincarnating the dead.

One of my favorite quotes about the potential reincarnation of the physical self comes from the novel *The Gods are Athirst*, by Anatole France. In the book, a character has been sentenced to the guillotine during the French Revolution and begins saying his final goodbyes to his fellow prisoners. Seeking to hide his sadness and fear in a jocular tone, he says to one of the prisoners, "Good-bye, I go before you into the land of nowhere. I gladly return to Nature the atoms of my composition, only hoping she will make a better use of them for the future, for it must be owned she did not make much of a job of me." I love this quote because it reminds me that while I will never accomplish all the grand designs I hoped to achieve when I was younger, the atoms that make up my body, the very composition of who I am, will continue to survive after I die. Hopefully, after my demise, those atoms that were my body will find their way into new and even more amazing arrangements.

The version of reincarnation presented in this section doesn't seem all that satisfying—certainly not as satisfying as a traditional afterlife where your conscious thoughts and memories continue to exist after you die. In some ways, though, perhaps reincarnation of the inexpressible self would be preferable to a traditional afterlife. A large part of the desire for life after death comes from the desire to never be forgotten. We all want to believe that our lives are meaningful—that we will leave a mark on this world, and that after we die, we will be remembered. In a traditional afterlife we would just be one of a billion other people who had once lived, less important and more ignored than the most famous people who had once drawn air. With reincarnation, though, we are all equal. Simply by being alive every one of us causes ripples to spread out through the universe, and we all equally influence the future. If every action you take, and every thought you have, helps decide the outcome of events for the rest of time, the universe itself will remember you.

Living For Reincarnation

How should you live your life, knowing that your thoughts and actions will reverberate through time? The answer to this question is very different from the answer given in Chapter 3 describing the block universe. In a block universe, every moment of time exists simultaneously; therefore, you should try to make each moment as enjoyable as possible because the you in that moment will experience that slice of time for eternity. In a deterministic or adequately deterministic universe, though, we have no idea how our thoughts or actions in the present moment will affect events in the future. Cheating on your taxes today may help bring about world peace tomorrow. As there is no way to know how our actions will influence the future, we should instead focus on the present. We should strive to live moral lives not because it will influence the reincarnation of our inexpressible selves after we die, but because it helps make ourselves and others happier right now.

While reincarnation may appear to shirk its duty to provide us with moral and ethical guidance, we must remember that in a deterministic universe, we don't have the free will necessary to make moral or ethical decisions. If the events of the past completely determine the events of the future, then the moral arc of the life you lead—whether saint, villain, or somewhere in between—has already been decided. We should all strive to lead moral lives, as doing so seems to be the key to a happy life. But on the other hand, don't be too hard on yourself if you fall short of your ideals—the universe may have preordained every single one of your failures.

Ripples In The Universe

In a deterministic universe, whenever you do anything—take even the smallest action—you are incising into the fabric of the universe in tall letters, "I was here!" When you throw a rock into a pond, the ripples spread out until they hit the bank of the shore and stop. In space there is no bank, no boundary, so the ripples of your actions continue to spread until the end of time. From these ripples are born the continual reincarnation of your inexpressible self.

The mark you can leave in a deterministic universe comes with a steep downside, though—in a deterministic universe, you do not have free will. It hurts the ego a bit to suppose that our sense of free will is illusory. On the other hand, we should feel comforted to know that our worst mistakes and most foolish decisions may have been determined thousands of years ago before the human species even evolved. To go even further, our worst mistakes were not our mistakes alone, as they could not have occurred without the billions of humans who lived before us and helped decide everything we would ever say, do, or think. Conversely, we should also feel humbled to realize that our greatest achievements and wisest pronouncements were also determined thousands of years before, and were directly attributable to those who lived before us. While humbling, we should feel proud that through reincarnation of our inexpressible selves, we will help bring about every great achievement that happens on Earth from our deaths until the end of time.

CHAPTER 9

GOD DOES NOT EXIST . . . YET

There are several myths describing the birth of the god Quetzalcoatl. One version has him being born from the earth-goddess Coatlicue, who also gave birth to four hundred other children who eventually formed the stars of the Milky Way. Another account has him being born from the virgin Chimalman after she swallowed an emerald. The version that definitely makes the most biological sense says that the god Mixcoatl shot an arrow that hit Chimalman in the womb, causing her to give birth to Quetzalcoatl nine months later.

In the Nahuatl language, Quetzalcoatl means feathered serpent (see Figure 9). In Aztec tradition, Quetzalcoatl was the god of Venus, also known as the morning star, and was therefore a symbol of death and rebirth. Not surprisingly for such an important god, Mesoamerican cultures had many stories involving Quetzalcoatl. In one tale, the god Tezcatlipoca

Figure 9. A representation of the feathered serpent god Quetzalcoatl, from the sixteenth century. Depicted in the *Codex Magliabechiano*, public domain.

persuaded Quetzalcoatl to get drunk on pulque. While Quetzalcoatl was drunk, Tezcatlipoca tricked him into having sex with his own sister, Quetzalpetlatl, who was a celibate priestess. The next morning, upon discovering what he had done, Quetzalcoatl was so ashamed that he instructed his servants to build a large chest. When it was completed, Quetzalcoatl lay down in the chest and set himself on fire. After the fire had killed him, Quetzalcoatl's ashes rose into the sky to become the morning star.

The Aztecs considered Quetzalcoatl a god, but certainly a very different kind of god from the one many of us recognize from the monotheistic religions. In the Aztec tradition, Quetzalcoatl was born and died, could get drunk and be tricked, and could feel shame for his actions. This raises an important question: Just how special do you have to be before you get to call yourself a god?

Defining God

The monotheistic religions, such as Christianity and Islam, conceive of God as all-knowing, all-present, all-powerful, and just an all-around supreme guy. If we accept this as the definition of God, then it makes sense that only one deity at a time could fit the description.

As Quetzalcoatl shows, though, to be a god in some cultures a being need not be all-powerful. Different cultures throughout history have had very different definitions for their gods. Several religions contain multiple gods that act as the divine movers behind such phenomena as rain, fertility, or death. These polytheistic religions often contain a plethora of gods, such as gods of the moon, the air, or the earth itself. Conversely, deist religions hold that a single god created the universe, establishing all its physical laws, but then walked away and has done nothing to influence the universe since then. Pantheistic religions take the definition of god the furthest, concluding that the entire universe exists as part of one single all-encompassing god. The definition of a god may range from a divine being that has power to cause certain natural events, all the way up to a god that encompasses the universe itself.

From these definitions of god, we can begin to form our own definition for use in this chapter. A first stab may define a god as a being that has power greater than that of any human. Unfortunately, this first attempt is obviously insufficient—if we ever come across aliens from other planets that can run faster, jump higher, or think better than we can, we would have to classify them as gods. Instead, I will propose a slightly more exclusive definition. For the purposes of this chapter, I define a god as any being that has power greater than that of any human, and whose power exists outside the known laws of nature.

Defining a god as having at least some extraordinary powers doesn't mean we have to assume that the god is all-powerful. For example, the ability to instantaneously teleport across the solar system may make a being a god under our definition; but when that god jumps across the solar system, we have no reason to suppose it can survive in the 880-degree Fahrenheit heat of Venus, or stay alive breathing only carbon dioxide. In other words, our teleporting god better have an ability to navigate that also exists outside the laws of nature if it wants to survive for very long.

The image of a god choking to death on the surface of Venus raises an important point—just because we define a being as a god, we have no reason to assume that such a god exists for eternity. There is no reason that a god may not come into existence by being born, and then go out of existence by dying.

At first it seems strange to think of a god as dying, but the Aztecs had no problem conceiving of Quetzalcoatl killing himself. Several other cultures have also told stories of their gods dying. In Norse mythology, the god Baldr died when he was pierced with a spear made of mistletoe—the only object on Earth that could harm him. In Egyptian mythology, the god Osiris was murdered by his brother Set, who then took his throne.

Just as gods may die, gods may also be born. As previously mentioned, Quetzalcoatl had several birth stories. The Greek god Zeus was born from the goddess Rhea and her brother Cronus. The Egyptian God Horus was born of the goddess Iris after she restored the body of her husband Osiris, allowing him to posthumously conceive their son. Given all the gods invented over the eons, and given how many had stories telling of their birth, we can safely wager that most gods throughout history were born at some point. We should therefore add that our definition of god does not preclude the entity from being born or from dying.

The Past And Future God

The concept of an all-powerful god that has always existed and will always exist is a relatively new one. As the previous section suggests, compared to the gods in most cultures, the idea of an all-powerful god is an anomaly. Instead of a supreme being, what if we consider the possibility of a lesser deity?

I want to begin this section by reiterating that despite millennia of looking, no philosopher or scientist has found evidence that god—any god—exists. While only a fool would state anything with absolute certainty, I can write with something pretty darn close that god, under almost any definition of such a being, does not exist. But I must concede that this certainty extends only to the present. While there may be no evidence of a god existing now, perhaps a god or gods existed billions of years ago but then ceased to exist for some unknowable reason. If a god existed billions of years ago and was constantly changing the universe to suit its whims, but then suddenly died, the evidence of that god's existence would have long ago faded. After the passage of so many years we would be unlikely to notice any telltale signs of a god's interference in the universe.

The main argument against a god existing in the past springs from a trifling little detail called the known laws of the universe. The laws of physics provide no reason to suspect that a god has ever existed, as scientists can explain the evolution of the universe without resorting to divine intervention. Additionally, there are no physical theories predicting that any power—divine or otherwise—existed outside of the natural laws of the universe in the distant past.

More importantly, even if a god did exist in the past but somehow died, it would not help the thesis of this book. The brief existence of a god billions of years ago would mean we couldn't rely on this no-longer-existing deity to grant us an afterlife.

More intriguing than the possibility of a god existing in the past is the possibility of a god existing in the future. While it seems fairly self-evident that a god does not exist now, that does not mean that a god will not eventually come into existence. We may feel confident in arguing that since a god does not currently exist, we should not expect such a deity to suddenly appear in the future. Humans, however, are notoriously poor at predicting the future. To explore why a god may suddenly pop into existence millions or billions of years from now, we first need to understand entropy.

Entropy

Scientists define entropy as a measure of the disorder of a system. For instance, a deck of Go Fish cards stacked in a neat pile has relatively low entropy. Those same Go Fish cards, thrown across the room by a four-year-old upset that he lost a game to his older brother, has much higher entropy because of the disordered nature in which the cards fall to the ground after hitting the wall.

The physics of Go Fish cards falls squarely within the second law of thermodynamics, which states that in an isolated system, entropy does not decrease over time. This means that entropy will usually increase with time, although in some rare circumstances it may remain the same. In other words, systems become more disordered as time passes. As the name suggests, the isolated system referenced in the second law of thermodynamics is one that remains isolated from its surroundings, exchanging neither heat nor work with the environment. Systems that aren't isolated may decrease in entropy, as long as the total entropy in the surrounding environment increases.

As an example of a non-isolated system that decreases in entropy, consider your house or apartment during the summer. If you live someplace that gets hot during the summer, then you likely have an air conditioner. When the air conditioner turns on, it cools the air in your house, thereby reducing the entropy of that air. However, the heat that the air conditioner generates in the process of cooling your house results in an increase in entropy in the environment greater than the decrease in entropy in the house. The result is a net increase of entropy in the environment (which is reflected in the size of the energy bill you pay at the end of the month!) Living organisms, including humans, are another example of non-isolated systems that can decrease their entropy by increasing the net entropy of the environment. As living beings, humans have relatively low entropy. We maintain that low entropy, though, by increasing the net entropy of the environment through doing things such as eating food, breathing in oxygen, and breathing out carbon dioxide. Ultimately, the environment that holds us all is the universe. The second law of thermodynamics tells us that the entropy of the universe—the disorder of the universe—will never decrease with time.

As defined above, entropy is a measure of the disorder of a system. Shifting our perspective, though, we can think of entropy in a very different way. We may conceive of entropy as a measure of the ways in which a system can be arranged. In other words, entropy is not merely a measure of disorder, it is also a measure of possibility.

Let's return to the Go Fish cards. Imagine the cards once again arranged in a nice low-entropy stack. A standard Go Fish deck has fifty-two cards, and after shuffling a bit, the individual cards may occur in any order in the stack. A bit of math shows that the deck of cards may be arranged in 8×10^{67} (an 8 followed by 67 zeroes) different ways. To put this in perspective, 8×10^{67} is larger than the total number of atoms on Earth. Stop and consider that this huge number is the low-entropy arrangement of the cards.

Now imagine the cards have been thrown against the wall. Some of the cards will land facing up while others land facing down; some will be stacked on top of one another while others lie alone. A few of the cards will end up leaning against the wall, while a couple may find themselves in the next room over. Clearly, the number of possible arrangements for a deck of fifty-two cards after they have been thrown against the wall will be much, much larger than the number of possible arrangements for the cards simply stacked one on top of another. I wouldn't want to make a guess, but the number of possible arrangements for the cards after having been thrown against the wall will certainly be greater than the number of atoms on Earth, and probably greater than the number of atoms in the universe. Put another way, the cards being thrown against the wall increases the entropy of the cards, but also vastly increases the possible arrangements of those cards.

The most likely arrangement for the cards after being thrown against the wall is a random, disordered mess. Imagine, however, a four-year-old throwing the cards against the wall hundreds or thousands of times. Almost every single time, the cards will land on the floor in a jumbled clutter. On occasion, though, the cards may land in an arrangement that appears to us as something other than a meaningless heap. A few of the cards may happen to fall by accident into a shape reminiscent of a happy face. Other times the cards may land in the shape of a horse, or appear to spell out a word. If thrown enough times, we may even see several of the cards fall in such a way as to create a house of cards two or three feet high.

If some of the cards do fall in such a way that they form a house of cards, we can properly conclude that those individual cards are in a low-entropy arrangement. Most of the other cards thrown against the wall, however, will have fallen into disordered positions on the floor. As a result, even though some of the cards may have randomly fallen into a house of cards, the overall entropy of the system will still be higher after the cards have been thrown against the wall than when they were stacked in a neat pile.

I took this tour through the workings of entropy to show that while scientists define entropy as a measure of disorder, increases in entropy also allow the formation of wonderous designs. While the total number of different possible arrangements of the Go

Fish cards stacked in a tidy deck is amazing, the cards are still only stacked in a deck. The process of throwing them against the wall, and thereby increasing their entropy, allows for a huge number of new arrangements. While most of those arrangements will result in a random jumble of cards on the floor, occasionally the cards may fall into a truly remarkable arrangement.

The arrangement of cards in a deck may seem interesting, but closer to a high school math problem than a phenomenon that can shed light on the workings of the universe. The ability of increases in entropy to reveal new possibilities, however, helps explain the origin of life on Earth. Immediately after the big bang, the universe was in a high-density, uniform state that had very low entropy. As the universe began to expand after the big bang, the entropy of the universe also increased (and has been increasing ever since). Tiny fluctuations in the early universe allowed particles of gas to coalesce, eventually forming stars. These stars then came together to form galaxies, and the births and deaths of the stars allowed the formation of rocky planets. On one of these rocky planets (much later called Earth), molecules were randomly bouncing into each other. At some point enough molecules happened to bounce into each other in just the right way, and came together to form the first life on Earth.

None of this could have occurred, though, if the universe were still in its initial low-entropy state. In the dense uniformity of the universe right after the big bang, life as it exists on Earth could not have formed. If the universe had remained in that state, there would be no galaxies or planets or life. The ever-increasing entropy of the universe allowed humans to come into being.

Entropy And God

Besides allowing humans to exist, entropy may also allow gods to exist. As explained in the last section, entropy measures not just disorder and randomness, but also possibility. Perhaps no god currently exists because it is not yet possible for a god to exist. With each passing second, the entropy of the universe increases, meaning that the possible states of the universe also increase. Much like throwing cards against the wall until a house of cards falls into place, perhaps we must simply wait until the random disorder of the universe allows a god to finally be born.

This idea puts the history of the universe as recounted by most religions on its head. In most religious traditions, a god exists before the universe is formed. The god, presumably out of sheer boredom, then causes the creation of the universe. This order of events, though, may be completely backward. I am arguing in this chapter that the universe already exists and did not need God to create it; instead, perhaps God needs a universe to create him.

How could the universe give birth to a god? Amidst swirling disorder, a god may simply pop into existence. The cards thrown against the wall become a house of cards, and the movement of the universe becomes a god. The weakness in such a premise rests in the fact that we have no evidence for anything even nearing the complexity of a god simply popping into existence. In the last several hundred years of scientific advancement, there is no record of a lump of matter, much less a divine being, simply appearing out of thin air. On the other hand, just because we haven't observed something happening on Earth in the last two hundred years doesn't mean it couldn't happen within the billions of years and billions of light years that make up the universe.

Instead of popping into existence fully formed, however, a being or species could evolve into a god over time. It took more than 3.5 billion years for life on Earth to evolve into human beings. On some planet, millions of light years from Earth, an alien species may be currently living and evolving. While humans as a group are pretty smart and have quite a few talents, there is no reason to assume that we have reached the pinnacle of intelligence or ability possible in the cosmos. The entropy that allowed the evolution of the human species may allow an alien species to evolve into gods.

Some readers may protest that while higher entropy does mean more possibilities, entropy is ultimately a measure of disorder. Consequently, as the number of possibilities increases, the proportion of those possibilities that are disordered and meaningless will also increase. When throwing the Go Fish cards against the wall, the probability of some of those cards falling in just the right way to form a house of cards is extremely small, while the probability of all of them landing in a meaningless jumble is much larger. Similarly, the likelihood of some truly amazing event, such as the birth of a god, will be so tiny as to not even be worth considering. Again, though, we must consider that while the birth of a god may be extremely unlikely, in a universe as incomprehensibly vast as the one we find ourselves in, the unlikely becomes likely. A god may yet be born.

Returning to the definition of a god I proposed for this chapter—a god must have some power that exists beyond the known laws of the universe. This presents an enormous hurdle for the possibility of the universe birthing a god. How could the natural phenomena of the universe give rise to the supernatural powers of a god? To answer this, let's look more closely at the possibility of an alien species evolving into gods.

The evolution of such an alien species might occur over millions of years, with each step in its evolution fitting entirely within the laws of physics. The result of that evolution, though, may be a species with an intelligence or abilities well beyond human capability. The intelligence and abilities of the alien species may appear to us as being so far beyond our understanding of the natural world as to be supernatural. In other words, an alien species may evolve in such a way as to attain the apparent supernatural powers of a god, even though those powers actually exist within the realm of scientifically discoverable laws. These powers may not truly fall outside the laws of nature, but to humans they would seem to be beyond those laws.

Before dismissing this argument as a bit of intellectual sleight of hand (or perhaps sleight of mind), reflect on what scientists in the nineteenth century would have considered the laws of nature. The physical laws would clearly state that a particle in one location could have no influence on a particle thousands of light years away. However, as hundreds of experiments have clearly shown, a particle may be entangled with another particle, and the state of the first particle will determine the state of the second particle. This quantum entanglement occurs even if both particles are separated by thousands of light years. To a scientist from the nineteenth century, quantum entanglement would clearly fall outside the laws of nature. Indeed, there are several other examples that I could use—quantum superpositions, black holes, even the technology required to build a computer chip—to show that what we take for granted today as part of the natural world would be entirely outside of the known laws of physics for a scientist living only 150 years ago.

Certainly, an alien species, evolving over millions of years along a very different trajectory from our own, may appear to us humans as having powers beyond the laws of nature. As Agatha Christie wrote in her 1933 short story, *The Hound of Death*, "The supernatural is only the natural of which the laws are not yet understood." More interestingly, though, is the possibility that the trajectory of an alien species's evolution may be so different from our own that we may be intellectually incapable of truly understanding its abilities. If an ability exists within the laws of nature, but humans are intellectually incapable of understanding those laws, then such an ability could only be described as belonging to a god. To amend Ms. Christie's quote, the supernatural is only the natural of which laws we are powerless to comprehend.

God And The Afterlife

If the universe does birth a god in the future, what does that mean for the possibility of an afterlife for humans living now? Unless a god happens to be born in the next day or two, chances are that such a deity will come into existence long after anyone living now has died. Does that mean that those of us alive at this moment will be left out of any potential life after death?

Not necessarily, as a god born in the future may decide to provide an afterlife for those living now. A god born in the future will by definition exist outside the laws of nature as we currently understand them. Perhaps one of the laws such a god could break would be the ability to travel through time. Our current understanding of physics seems to foreclose the ability to travel backward through time. Our future god, though, may be able to overcome this apparent law of nature.

Such a time-traveling god may also find itself with the ability to create an afterlife for the living beings that existed in the past. Again, this would be outside our current understanding of the laws of nature, but let us suppose a future god is born with such an ability. The god may decide that traveling through time to provide an afterlife for every being that has ever lived would be a worthwhile use of its supernatural powers. Indeed, every one of us living right now may find ourselves enjoying life after death, created by a god born billions of years in the future.

There are two main objections to this idea. The first comes from the time-traveling aspect—if a god travels back in time to give the humans living now an afterlife, then that means a god exists in the present moment. As mentioned several times throughout this book, no scientist or philosopher has ever presented any convincing evidence for the existence of a god in the present. If a god does exist right now, we would expect that god to alter the universe in ways outside the known laws of nature. In other words, if a god exists now, we should find unexplained phenomena that can only be explained by the existence of a god.

One could counter that a god could potentially exist in the present, but has decided to lie low, refusing to alter the universe. A god that exists now but refuses to meddle in the affairs of the universe, though, results in the exact same universe as no god existing. If a god exists but refuses to interact with the universe, we may as well continue to assume that no god exists.

This counter-argument, though, turns out a bit differently for a god born in the future. Such a god would certainly realize that if it traveled back through time and changed anything in the past, it would quite possibly prevent itself from being born. As discussed in Chapter Eight, the universe may be deterministic (or at least adequately deterministic), meaning that any event that occurs in the present happens only because of the events that occurred in the past. Any changes a god made before it was born could deterministically change the future, causing the god not to be born. Assuming our hypothetical god enjoys existing, it would not want to do anything to risk that existence. As a result, a god born in the future may be able to travel through time but would likely be very careful about not making any changes to the past.

Indeed, refusing to meddle in the universe may very well be a hallmark of the gods—after all, they don't want to risk their existence. A god traveling through time but refusing to alter anything would still be able to collect information on the beings who have lived in the past. Such a god, after collecting such information, could then decide to provide an afterlife for all those beings who have already died. This idea, however, brings us to the next objection.

The second objection to a god of the future creating an afterlife for those living now arises from the realization that we have absolutely no idea what goes on inside the mind of a god. We have no reason to believe that a god would have any desire to provide an afterlife to dead humans, much less a bunch of humans who died millions or billions of years before the god was even born. I made a similar argument in Chapter Two with regard to an alien species simulating our current world—we have no reason to assume that we can guess how an alien species, much less a deity, may think.

In the Christian tradition, believers assume God to be wholly good and compassionate, with never an immoral thought or action. The problem with such a belief, though, comes from admitting that what we humans consider moral and immoral changes through time—actions considered moral in the past are no longer thought moral today, while actions we consider moral now may be considered completely immoral in the future. Just as we condemn bearbaiting today, perhaps humans in the future will be absolutely disgusted to learn that their ancestors ate meat, or burned coal, or allowed anyone to appear on a reality TV show. Given the ever-evolving nature of morality and immorality, we simply have no clue what ideals a god would hold.

In fact, a god born in the future who had the power to grant every human an afterlife may consider such an act entirely *immoral*. Perhaps such a god would decide that reviving a formerly living being without their express consent to be a violation of that being's autonomy. Or perhaps the god would reason that any existence—even an existence in an afterlife as close to paradise as possible—would still contain suffering (even in paradise humans would somehow find a way to suffer). The god may then conclude that causing any increase in suffering within the universe constitutes an immoral act. Or most likely, a god born in the future simply wouldn't care about any beings who had died in the past, and would never even consider whether resurrecting such beings might be moral or immoral.

On the other hand, a god may be absolutely eager to resurrect dead humans. As conscious life on this planet illustrates, complexity likes complexity. Obviously, I cannot state this as a universal law of physics, but within the limited scope of animal life on Earth, as species become more mentally complex, they find complex phenomena more and more fascinating. If you show a lizard several works of art, the lizard will act as though they are not even there. Show those same works of art to Java Sparrows and they will perch in front of the art they prefer. Show those exact same works of art to human graduate students and you will get several fifty-page theses on the liminality of standing (or perching) before representational art and the syncretism of animal cultures in fairy-tale-inspired illustrations.

As the complexity of the animal mind increases, the interest in the complexity of the universe also increases. Quite possibly, any god that happens to exist would be very captivated by any complexity it can find. Hopefully, the complex mind of a god would be interested by, and place great value on, the complex minds of humans. If such a god did esteem the human mind, then possibly that god would resurrect those minds so that their complexity would continue to exist in the universe. Put another way, a god born in the future may find a way to give humans alive now an afterlife simply because doing so would make the cosmos a bit more fascinating.

Uncertainty

I will admit to a great deal of uncertainty in including this chapter in the book. Suggesting in a book aimed at atheists and agnostics that while god does not exist now, such a deity may exist in the future, has likely caused quite a few readers to scoff and roll their eyes. Moreover, the suggestion that there may be laws of nature that science has not yet discovered, and that a god may someday exist who could exploit those laws, also invites ridicule.

However, I believe that we should all strive to acknowledge the uncertainty that constantly surrounds everything we think we know. Like a fog that allows you to clearly see the objects directly before you but obscures anything farther away, we may see our little bit of the universe clearly today, but the vast expanses of space and time obscure what we can see in the distance. The probability of a god being born somewhere in the universe is almost laughably small. At the same time, the likelihood of your birth, or my birth, or any birth, was also laughably small. God may not exist now, but maybe we should give the universe a few billion more years before we make up our minds that God can never exist.

CHAPTER 10

CONCLUSIONS

Most people who don't believe in God have several reasons for their disbelief—chief among them being the contention that belief in something as extraordinary as a God requires extraordinary proof. At this point in time, such extraordinary proof simply does not exist.

Any reader who requires extraordinary proof before accepting the existence of God will almost certainly require extraordinary proof before accepting the existence of the afterlife. Clearly, throughout this book I have failed. Neither science nor philosophy have found any incontrovertible proof for life after death. (No one should be surprised by this conclusion, because if I had discovered incontrovertible proof for the afterlife, I would almost certainly be leading my own major religion at the moment instead of writing this book, and that likely would have made the news.) However, this book was never meant to prove the existence of the afterlife—instead, this book was meant to provide several reasons to believe that such an afterlife could possibly exist. I hope that throughout these pages I have suggested eight plausible ways in which humans may enjoy life after death.

What Constitutes An Afterlife?

As discussed in several earlier chapters, the potential versions of the afterlife presented in this book do not always resemble the afterlife described by the major religions. When we think of the afterlife, we immediately imagine a paradise where we spend all our days utterly joyful and fulfilled. We also immediately imagine that our conscious minds and memories are intact in this paradise. As promised by most religions, in the afterlife we are essentially who we were in life, just much happier. Several of the chapters in this book suggest the possibility of just such an afterlife. Chapters Two and Five, for instance, argue that an advanced civilization could create a simulated afterlife that closely resembles the religious version of life after death.

Several other chapters in this book, though, posit a very different type of afterlife. For example, the block universe of Chapter Three describes an afterlife completely dissimilar from the religious version of life after death. In the block universe the afterlife consists of simultaneously existing in every moment of one's life for eternity. Conversely, Chapter Eight argues for reincarnation as a form of afterlife. The idea of reincarnation as life after death is even further removed from the religious view than the block universe. If any of the versions of life after death presented in this book are accurate, then the afterlife may be very different from what first pops into our heads when thinking about life after death. We should stop and consider, though, that just as there is more than one way to enjoy a happy life, perhaps there is more than one way to enjoy an afterlife.

The fact that the version of the afterlife we find easiest to imagine most closely resembles the religious one raises an important question: Why do so many of us hope for the religious version of the afterlife? What is it about fluffy clouds, benevolent angels, and our conscious minds existing forever that we find so appealing?

As seems to be the case for most things involving humans, the answer almost certainly comes down to our egos. I imagine the vast majority of us want our consciousness to continue on after death. Part of the reason resides in a fear of no longer existing, but a larger part has to do with a belief that each one of us secretly harbors that our particular mind is truly special. We each like to believe that it would be truly sad for the universe to lose such a marvelous consciousness as the one we happen to inhabit.

Because of this belief in the specialness of our own mind, an afterlife where our consciousness is not exactly the same as it is right now seems hollow. Consider whether you would be happy if your mind as a four-year-old was what ended up in the afterlife. You would consider it unfair that all the memories from after you were a child were forgotten. You might even go so far as to think that an afterlife for your four-year-old mind was meaningless. But the mind of four-year-old you is still your mind, still your consciousness (ignoring for the moment the ship of Theseus paradox from Chapter Six). Imagine instead that you are lucky enough to live to be one hundred years old. You might be disappointed if the version of you that ends up in the afterlife is the one-hundred-year-old version, though, with a mind slowed by age and memories dimmed by time. On the other hand, one-hundred-year-old you might think life after death a waste if the version that ends up in the afterlife is the version of you as you are right now.

On a fundamental level, it shouldn't matter which version of your mind ends up in the afterlife. After all, no matter how old you are, you are still you. But obviously it does matter, at least psychologically, because we all tend to think of the version of ourselves in the present moment as the "real" version. This realization makes the block universe form of the afterlife a bit more appealing. In the block universe, every single version of your mind exists for eternity, because every moment of your mind exists for eternity. Death does not get to choose which version of you makes it to the afterlife. The same holds true for reincarnation. The deterministic form of reincarnation described in Chapter Eight suggests that every thought you have, and every action you take, influences the universe for the rest of eternity. In this view of the afterlife, your conscious mind may not survive death, but the ripples emanating from your life keep expanding forever. Like the afterlife of the block universe, in a deterministic universe every moment of your life rests on an equal footing with every other moment in leaving a legacy within the cosmos.

The notion that only your conscious mind at the exact moment of your death gets to enjoy the afterlife places too great a privilege on that one moment in time. The versions of the afterlife described by the block universe and reincarnation begin with the presumption that all the moments of your life—every single moment of conscious thought—are equal. No second of your life deserves the afterlife more than any other. This view of the afterlife seems much more meaningful than the traditional religious view. Doesn't every moment of your life, every past, present, and future you, deserve life after death?

Several forms of the afterlife described in this book seem at first to fall short of the religious-inspired paradise we might imagine. Hopefully, however, we can accept a different version of the afterlife as no less meaningful than the traditional religious one. In fact, a nontraditional afterlife might be preferable, as it would give weight and significance to every single second of your life.

But Do We Really Want Life After Death?

I have been assuming throughout this book that most of us would be happy to discover that some form of the afterlife awaits us upon death. We should stop and consider, though, whether we are wise to desire *any* version of the afterlife. Are there downsides to life after death?

Consider first the traditional religious view of the afterlife. As previously mentioned, the possibility of such an afterlife was taken up in Chapters Two and Five as resulting from computer simulations run by advanced civilizations. In such a traditional afterlife, our conscious minds would be resurrected, and we would live in a paradise free from pain or sickness. We would also likely enjoy complete leisure to pursue whatever activities happened to pique our interests. We would never know hardship or want, and never need to overcome any hindrance. If such an afterlife exists, we may find ourselves experiencing it for millions or billions of years, or maybe even for all eternity.

In such a marvelous paradise, how long before life after death gets stupefyingly boring? After a few million years we would surely experience every experience even the most beautifully crafted paradise has to offer. We would have read all the books that have ever been written, seen every play that has ever been produced, eaten every food that has ever been cooked, and taken every drug that has ever been concocted. Quite likely, the constant companion of eternal existence would be eternal boredom.

More importantly, there would be no sense of meaning in a paradisiacal afterlife. Humans tend to find purpose only when faced with an obstacle that must be overcome. By its very definition, in paradise there would be no obstacles. Perhaps a psychologically adept programmer would create some hardships for the humans in the afterlife to face; but they would be illusory obstacles, providing illusory purpose and meaning. Zookeepers often give the captive gorillas in their care fruit frozen in blocks of ice. The gorillas have to work a bit to get the fruit free from the ice, giving them something to do during the long days in their enclosures. I imagine the gorillas would rather be in the wild, overcoming real hardships rather than the ones well-meaning humans made up to keep them occupied. The same would certainly be true of any contrived obstacles created for us to overcome in paradise. We may begin to resent the very people who created the afterlife for us. The inescapable state of life after death could be ennui—the afterlife making French philosophers of us all.

The same caution applies to the other versions of the afterlife described in this book. As discussed in Chapter Three, an afterlife in the block universe means that a version of you experiences the absolute worst moment of your life for all eternity. Perhaps this can be balanced by the version of you experiencing the best moment of your life for all time, but the version experiencing the worst moment may not consider it a fair trade-off. Similarly, if reincarnation exists, maybe I would prefer that not every moment of my life influences every other living being on Earth. I'm not sure that thinking about picking my nose (or giving in to picking my nose) needs to ripple forever through time, influencing the universe for eternity. To put this another way, most of what us humans do every day is boring and meaningless, and it does not seem necessary that every single one of our thoughts and actions continue on after we are dead.

And yet, despite the potential ennui or nose-based wrinkles of the afterlife, I imagine most of us would still prefer life after death over resolute, unalterable demise. Perhaps we are optimistic enough to hope that the afterlife will be a marvelous new adventure, even if there are moments that are less than perfect. Or more likely, our fear of eternal oblivion dwarfs our fear of eternal boredom. Either way, yearning for an afterlife seems natural for most of us, and while the afterlife may end up being less like paradise and more like a trip to a doctor's waiting room, at least your mind will still exist—your thoughts and memories not yet lost to the universe.

The Fairy Tales We Tell

Despite the hope many of us harbor that life continues after death, to return to the beginning of this chapter, we must remain wary about the lack of proof for any version of the afterlife. To hold that God does not exist because we can find no proof, but then to turn around and believe in life after death, seems downright comical. For many of us who consider ourselves atheists, believing in God is little better than believing in fairy tales. We do not believe in the existence of the Pied Piper simply because a story exists about him in a book. How is believing in the afterlife any different? A belief in the afterlife seems to amount to nothing more than a belief in fairy tales, perhaps gilded by a few scientific or philosophical ideas that do little to support the weight of proving life after death.

But fairy tales are told in chronological order. In fact, the vast majority of stories are told in chronological order, with time flowing in one direction from beginning to middle to end. The flow of time is so ingrained in our understanding of the universe we take it completely for granted. Even in the Bible, God— described as omnipotent and omnipresent—doesn't go mucking about with the order of time.

Our intuitive understanding of time is important because it means that the hope for an afterlife is really a hope to overcome the flow of time. Like a story, we perceive our lives to move from beginning to middle to end. We yearn for something to come after the end, but fear the odds are slim because time does not work that way. As Chapter Three suggested, though, experiment after experiment has demonstrated that time does not simply flow in a nice straight line. The flow of time is never steady, with the order of events not even fixed. If time does not flow in a perfectly straight line, perhaps the end is not truly the end. If the story of your life does not flow from beginning to middle to end, then perhaps there is no end, only beginning after beginning.

Despite a general acceptance of the weirdness of the universe, cynicism remains the easiest option. It would be very simple to assume that because God does not exist, the afterlife does not exist, and that anyone who argues otherwise is either fooling himself or merely a fool. I certainly had to fight with my cynical side the entire time I was writing this book. On multiple occasions this entire project seemed downright silly. But then I would stumble on a brilliant scientific idea I was unfamiliar with, or go for a walk and stare up at a beautiful blue sky, and I would realize just how little I know and how just how shallow is the depth of my experience.

I have attempted to illustrate in this book that there are many different forms the afterlife may take, and that the paths to those distinct versions of life after death are grounded in observable phenomena. Put another way, while there may not be definitive proof of life after death, there are scientific and philosophical suggestions that show that the idea is far from outlandish. There may not be any gods, but the universe has never needed any gods to surprise us.

I conclude this book by reminding you that it is easy to by cynical, to revel in being hardheaded and analytical, but much more difficult to be open to the possibility of a world beyond what we know. I have no idea if the afterlife exists, but I am willing to soften my cynical side enough to entertain the idea that it could. Hopefully you are also willing to at least consider the possibility that the end of your life is not the end of your existence, and that an afterlife awaits us all.

ABOUT THE AUTHOR

Sea Kimbrell writes from his home in Kansas. He has a JD and a PhD in biology, but only because he likes scribbling lots of letters after his name. Sea is also the author of the novel, *Be the Good Lamb*.

NOTES

[1] Lawson, Carol. "Tamagotchi: Love It, Feed It, Mourn It." *The New York Times* (May 22, 1997).

[2] Grimm, David. "Research on lab chimps is over. Why have so few been retired to sanctuaries?" *Science* (June 12, 2017).

[3] This example adapted from *emc2-explained*, www.emc2-explained.info.

[4] Hameroff, Stuart, and Deepak Chopra. "The 'Quantum Soul': A Scientific Hypothesis." A. Moreira-Almeida and F.S. Santos (eds.), *Exploring Frontiers of the Mind-Brain Relationship, Mindfulness in Behavioral Health.* (Springer, 2012).

[5] Freeman, Dyson J. *Dear Professor Dyson: Twenty Years of Correspondence Between Freeman Dyson and Undergraduate Students on Science, Technology, Society and Life.* Dwight E. Neuenschwander (ed.), (World Scientific Publishing Co. Pte. Ltd., 2016).

[6] Searle, John R. "Minds, brains, and programs." *Behavioral and Brain Sciences*, 3:417-457 (1980).

[7] Swinburne, Richard. *Is There a God (Revised Edition)*, (Oxford University Press, 1996).

[8] *Id.*

Made in the USA
Monee, IL
29 January 2022